LIFE
IS NOT
A LONG
QUIET
RIVER

To ~~John~~ & Cecile
ŵ much love

Willy

LIFE IS NOT A LONG QUIET RIVER

A Memoir

WILLY SLAVIN

BIRLINN

For the Sisters

First published in 2019 by
Birlinn Limited
West Newington House
10 Newington Road
Edinburgh
EH9 1QS

www.birlinn.co.uk

ISBN: 978 1 78027 578 9

British Library Cataloguing-in-Publication Data
A catalogue record for this book is available from the British Library

Typeset by Initial Typesetting Services, Edinburgh
Printed and bound by Gutenberg Press, Malta

Grow old along with me!
The best is yet to be,
The last of life, for which the first was made:
Our times are in His hand
Who saith, 'A whole I planned,
Youth shows but half; trust God: see all nor be afraid!'

– 'Rabbi Ben Ezra', Robert Browning

Contents

Part 3

Celibacy

Introduction

Written almost 3,000 years ago is a line from a song in the Bible which says: 'The days of our lives are 70 years'. Not everyone remembers the next line, which notes the possibility, 'by reason of strength', of 80 years (Psalm 90:10, New King James Version). This is a bald statistic, but it is an average, subject to the usual variation. Some will make it to 90 or 100, maybe a little more. Others will get only 50 or 60 years, perhaps even less. Genetic inheritance, infection, accident, violence or suicide can cut the promised span.

Ageing is still associated with certain health problems – strokes, cancer, dementia. This is not because we are living too long. These problems are not intrinsic to ageing – many older people die without being affected by them, and gradually modern medicine is dealing with them. Those who have already reached 70 or 80 in good health are pioneers. This is what the psalm promises. It is a message to be celebrated; it should be proclaimed in our society, and needs to be taken to those parts of the world where infection and violence are still endemic. Older people, far from being a burden, are completing the natural human life cycle. This is not a matter only of chronological measurement – if you didn't know your date of birth, how old would you think you are?

There is the objection that ageing is a descent into a second childhood. While we are children, we have to do what we are told; we don't have money of our own; we know nothing of sex. Is a return to that kind of life – dependent, poor, single – still worth living?

As we grow up we are proud to stand on our own two feet, wanting to get our own way, taking pleasure in our first pocket money, feeling the first stirrings of psychosexual development. When we become adults we are encouraged to find a path in the world; a job gives us independence; friendship and intimacy beckon. Traditional marriage vows include a promise of obedience, the sharing of wealth and fidelity, forsaking sex with others. However, in order to keep a job, people constantly have to fit in with the expectations of others, if not through obedience then through loyalty or conformity. For most of our lives we have not wealth but debt, a mortgage being the most acute example. *Mort-gage* means 'pledged until death'. Despite the surfeit of sex in the media, most couples try to be faithful to each other.

We are destined to end life the way we started. Sooner or later we will have to obey others, perhaps even our own children. In old age we have a diminished income and are not able to spend very much, at least on ourselves. We may live alone or have to face – for better and for worse – life with strangers, without kith or kin.

Not to put too fine a point on it, many of us end up as obedient, poor and celibate as monks, nuns or whatever is the equivalent in different traditions. A Hindu idea is that we should put our affairs in order before we make our final journey, hoping to be fit enough to complete the traditional trek to the Ganges before we are laid on the funeral pyre and our ashes are scattered upon the waters. Rather than abandoning ourselves to simply having to pass the time in old age, we should put more effort into preparing for it.

Cryogenics notwithstanding, who wants to live forever? Despite the provision of new knees and hips, stents and shunts, Botox and Viagra, our bodies will come to a natural end. Our eyes, ears and teeth tell us this. Bits will degrade. To ask more would be inhuman. We are born unable to do anything for ourselves, completely dependent on others. We die in the same way. To treat the time in between as being only for eating, drinking and having a good time is the vanity of vanities. Our bodies are not designed only for conforming, consuming and consummating.

It is tempting to treat the body as a machine. Many parts can be renewed or replaced. But there is more to life than the mechanisms of the body which allow us to realise our dreams, to make money, to have sex. No matter how rational people think themselves to be, in fact they do the most irrational things: the most intelligent can be selfish, greedy and lose their self-control. Biographies, to say nothing of court records, demonstrate this.

The 1988 French satirical film *La vie est un long fleuve tranquille*

(Life Is a Long Quiet River) begins in Paris with the stylish mother of a large bourgeois family teaching Catholic catechism alongside a young guitar-playing priest. Then she finds out that, 12 years previously, one of her children was swapped at birth and has been brought up in a poor family on the other side of the tracks. She and her husband agree to take the boy back while paying the poor family to keep the one they have brought up. But the 12-year-old has learned all the tricks required to survive in the slums. These include stealing and drinking. Soon he has his new-found, and hitherto well-behaved, brothers and sisters imitating his bad example. The mother, distraught, starts swallowing liquor and popping pills. One day, one comes to tell her what he has been learning in school. 'Maman,' he says, 'Jesus was a good man. And he got crucified. Maman, life is not a long quiet river.'

The Ancient Greek philosopher Socrates said 'the unexamined life is not worth living'. These days, as we age, we have the opportunity to examine our lives; our retirement plans should include time to be alone, silent, contemplative. During the 'extra' decade that falls roughly between 70 and 80, we can more easily see the bigger picture and how our lives fit into it. The premise of this book is that those years are not designed only for rest and recreation. They are for reflection on what our existence has been all about. We need to understand not only the benefits but also the limitations of power, money and sex. Monks and nuns give up their own will and property, renouncing sex and comfort. Perhaps we should all attempt this. As T.S. Eliot says, in *Four Quartets*: 'East Coker', 'In order to possess what you do not possess / You must go by the way of dispossession.'

This book has three sections, dedicated respectively to obedience, poverty and celibacy. They cover the stages of a life – my own – from birth to old age, facing at each stage the challenges that have come from trying to live in the world as a Roman Catholic priest. Priests are not just cogs in an institution; they are called to live according to the Gospel of Jesus Christ. This 'good-spell' questions why the majority of people have to survive without choices so that a minority can live in peace. Since priests don't exercise choices that others regard as routine, they should be free to speak up on behalf of those in the family of humanity who have no voice at all.

These thoughts are offered to those seeking to complete their lives 'grace-fully'. I have kept diaries and notes from an early age. From these I have concluded that the so-called 'evangelical' or Gospel virtues – obedience, poverty and chastity – can give a fuller meaning to life. We are all more obedient, poor and celibate than we care to admit, but when we use our 'extra' decade from 70 to 80 to reflect upon our life, we discover that we are not merely stardust destined only to fertilise the earth. This is the age at which I chose to leave the city and move to a hut in the woods. Some of those who visit the hut betray a certain envy. We have all, in our older age, far too much stuff. It is time to dispense with most of it and focus on that which remains – our selves.

For those thinking of writing a memoir, it is worth considering the words of R.B. Cunninghame Graham: 'Why strip the soul stark naked to the public gaze without some hesitation and due interval, by means of which to make folk understand that which you write is what you think you feel; part of yourself, a part, moreover, which once given out can never be recalled?'

What I have written is what I have felt during the extra decade. Hopefully the reader will have felt something similar. Sooner or later we all have to face the same issues. If we have obtained a degree of satisfaction with the life we have led then we are entitled to contentment. It only remains to complete the cycle of life with grace-fulness.

Part 1
Obedience

1

Birth

Although I think of myself as Scottish, I was born in England. My parents happened to be there at the time. My father's father had been a master potter in the world-famous Belleek Pottery in Ulster. He had been invited to the Blue Pottery in Glasgow, where he met Jean Macauley, whose family origins were in Stornoway. They had seven boys (of whom my father was the second) and two girls. My mother came from a family of six girls and one boy. Her name was Sarah but she was known as Sadie or, because of her lack of height, 'Tote' (Scots for tiny). Her mother died in childbirth and the children were brought up in a large flat in Springburn by their father, Felix McCann, a signalman at nearby Cowlairs Junction. The family traced their origins to the Irish who came over after the 1840s 'Great Hunger' as labour in the brickworks at Heathfield near Garnkirk in Lanarkshire. I think of my mother as a Catholic Calvinist: she was strong on the work ethic. An uncle described her as 'very religious'. She trained as a pawnbroker and later opened a draper's shop. She taught us to say our prayers each night by our bedside. Some prayers were learned off by heart, and we were encouraged to remember friends and neighbours.

My father had mistakenly been called up for the First World War – he often told us of his delight in pointing out to the recruiting sergeant that he was too young. He remembered the man calling him a cheeky young pup as he flicked back the king's shilling. He qualified in the 1920s as an engineer at the North British Locomotive works in Springburn, Glasgow. With 8,000 employees, it was the biggest railway builder in the British Empire, sending steam engines all over the world. There are iconic photographs of them being lifted onto ships in the River Clyde by the enormous Finnieston crane. The company custom was to dismiss apprentices as soon as their time was up, so that they could avoid paying full wages – so, as he came from a musical family, instead of pursuing an engineering career in Glasgow, my father set himself to become a professional pianist. He was soon leading a small band that played in a city-centre café. He also became a first-class oil and watercolour artist, producing paintings that contributed to the household budget. However, when he proposed marriage to my mother she told him she would not consider bringing up children on such an unpredictable income. In anticipation of another war, engineering work was picking up in England, and friends got him a start in the Bristol Aeroplane Company, where their factory in Filton was the largest aircraft facility in Europe.

The River Thames froze over for the first time since 1888 on the day of my birth in 1940. This was followed by an ice storm. Things only got worse: Bristol suffered badly from German bombing because of the aerodrome beside which we lived. Over 1,000 civilians were killed and 81,000 houses destroyed. My father would run from the air-raid shelter to the house to heat milk for me. He felt, he told me later, part of the 'spirit of Dunkirk'. War production increased and Rolls-Royce opened an aircraft division in Glasgow. He transferred, reckoning the family might be safer there. So although both my sister (two years older) and my brother (two years younger) were also born in England, we were brought up in Scotland.

My father regarded his Catholicism as a healthy antidote to the attractions of Communism which, after the Russian Revolution of 1917, was a significant influence in Glasgow. The Gaelic poet Sorley MacLean wrote of 'the great cause' and of 'a new star lit in heaven'. The family locale of Springburn was a particular bastion of the Communist Party. 'Wee Johnny', as my father was known, was in George Square when strikers gathered there in 1919. They were fighting for a reduction of the working week from 54 hours to 40. Churchill, the Secretary of State for War, was blamed for ordering in armed troops to quell the spread of what the Secretary of State for Scotland called a 'Bolshevik uprising'. When a tram was overturned, young Johnny ran all the way home.

The parish priest in Springburn, Canon McBrearty, regarded the Slavin family as 'brainy but arrogant'. Two of my father's brothers did veterinary surgery at Glasgow University and both went on to Leipzig for further studies. Another brother emigrated to New York and one became a Justice of the Peace in Glasgow.

As a parent, my father was much more laid-back than my mother, and softened her discipline. Children should be free to express themselves, he thought. The nearest he got to discipline was a knuckle touching the top of the head with the admonition to 'do what Mammy tells you'.

In those years children were seen and not heard. They tended to accept their parents' opinions as Gospel truth – and my father was free with his opinions. His hero was Clement Attlee, the post-war Labour prime minister who nationalised the public utilities. His greatest enemy was a somewhat mythical Duke of Argyll, to whom he attributed all Scotland's ills. He put down his lack of promotion to Masonic influence but he was a 'contrary' character. Once, having on a Sunday walked the requisite distance to a hotel to qualify for a drink as a bona fide traveller, he was asked to remove his cap. 'Why?' he asked. 'Is there going to be a religious service?'

From my father I inherited this contrariness. Power, prestige and position meant little to him. My mother, on the other hand, wanted her children to 'get on'. And she passed on her dogmatic tendencies. My parents remained in a certain sense independent of each other. When they disagreed about something my father would say to the three of us: 'A Hindu died / a happy thing to do / for forty years / he had been married to a shrew.' We laughed. Still, they were part of each other. They might have had a streak of anarchism about them. They trimmed their sails to let us fly. They might have hoped we would not fly too far, but they left that decision to us. Obedience, though not conformity, was taught as a virtue.

Being born into the working class provided the discipline necessary for growing up. 'Working class' can be misunderstood to mean mere factory fodder, but there were skilled occupations – such as engineers, coal miners and shipbuilders – of which the practitioners were justifiably proud. The world was ill-divided, but there were rules and regulations. If you obeyed these you would make progress. My parents were better off than their parents, and they worked hard to make sure their own children were better off than them. As they saw it, you could conform to social expectations enough to make a good living, but you should still keep your conscience clean and be your own person: you must remain obedient to what you believed in, no matter what you had to do to conform and get on.

2

Boyhood

I started primary school in 1945, in the month the atomic bombs were dropped on Hiroshima and Nagasaki. At enormous cost to all sides, the war was over. The name of our school was St George's. People ask how in Glasgow you could get a school called after England's patron saint. The parish priest, Canon 'Geordie' Galbraith from South Uist, called it after himself. He was the best-known priest in the city. He had a Military Cross from the First World War for 'dedicated duty under fire' while a chaplain with the Highland Light Infantry. Later he received the MBE. He insisted that the lamp posts which the Corporation of Glasgow painted green in the rest of the city be painted blue on the road to his church. This was the traditional colour of the Virgin Mary, patron of his parish of Our Lady of Lourdes. And the road had to be signposted not Lourdes Avenue but Lourdes Ave (for Ave Maria).

Miss Annie Campbell, one of two sisters from the island of Barra, was our teacher. She was a strict disciplinarian, believing that although all her pupils were working class there should be no limit to their aspirations. 'Education opens doors,' she said. In the Scottish Qualifying Examination for Secondary School our class received the highest marks in Glasgow. Miss Campbell died of cancer not long after we left primary school. Such was her influence that members of the class have continued to meet in her honour to the present day.

The school football team played in St George's colours, with red and white stripes. In my final year we reached the Glasgow Schools Cup Final. Since the parish was Our Lady and St George we were given a gift of blue socks, Mary's colour. The final was played on the park of a junior team, Maryhill Harp, which had Irish origins. When we ran out in red, white and blue we got a hostile reception and were 3–0 down before we rallied to 3–3, only to lose 4–3.

We were within walking distance of Ibrox Park, where we were lifted over the turnstiles for free to see epic encounters such as between the Rangers 'Iron Curtain' and Hibernian's 'Famous Five'. My father went with a busload of supporters from the Rolls-Royce factory to Wembley in 1949 to see Scotland beat England 3–1. He had also been at the Rangers–Celtic match in 1931 during which the Celtic goalkeeper John Thomson was fatally injured. He spoke of the silence when the Rangers manager came on to the pitch and the spectators realised the seriousness of the incident.

Most families where we lived in Penilee were connected through the employment of men in the Rolls-Royce plant, which had its own pipe band. We were intrigued by one of the drummers having a wooden leg, revealed by his kilt. Father was fit, and cycled to work. Time-keeping was strict, and we would sit at the window sure to the minute of his return, when we would run out to meet him. He didn't take factory work too seriously and referred to Rolls-Royce as 'Dodge City' – the tool crib in which he worked was regarded as a nest of 'bolshie' characters. He enjoyed telling us the story of an inspector coming up from Derby to check one of the first bits of automation. 'Can't that machine go any faster?' he boomed. 'Sure bloody thing,' said one of the engineers, turning it up to full speed and nearly wrecking it.

I was a member of the Cubs, where the leaders (called 'Akela', a Kipling character) were two sisters, idolised by the boys. We followed *Oor Wullie* and *The Broons*, cartoons of the most dysfunctional families imaginable, perhaps a safety valve in strict households. Bizarrely, although it was perhaps a similar safety valve, my father insisted on reading out to my mother 'Little Stories from the Police Courts' from the *Weekly News* on Friday evenings, in which downtrodden women got their own back on feckless husbands.

When we played far from home in summer the sun seemed always to shine, while winters were snowy – we were able to sledge in the field at the end of the street. In 1947 the snow came over our wellington boots and the school milk had to be thawed out on the classroom stove. Fog was a regular problem too, and occasionally it was impossible to see across the road. Our street led on to three farms, round which we walked of a Sunday. Of course, we went to church on Sundays too. Some people went to different places of worship. This was not experienced as sectarianism, despite the tensions between Catholics and Protestants in parts of Glasgow (I was 12 before I saw an Orange band).

There were two cinemas within walking distance. There was another we were not allowed to go to because the children threw stuff at each other. Occasionally we were taken by bus to the Lyceum, one of three 'picture houses' in Govan. We had to agree to go first to confession in St Anthony's Church across the street from the cinema. Our greatest delinquency – the only thing we could seriously confess to – was stealing chocolate from a biscuit factory in Hillington estate. There was a van came round weekly from the Band of Hope which showed films with a religious background. I once won a pencil at it but my mother snapped it in two since I wasn't supposed to be at a 'non-Catholic' service – a reminder that children should do what they were told.

There was no way of questioning the instructions of the various parental figures of childhood. Memory suggests that they were benign authorities. The school janitor, Mr Gilfedder, was more immediate to us than the headmaster. His word was law. It was assumed that he and others like him were interested only in our good. They made every effort to improve us. Children were cherished and protected. Parents, teachers, clergy and others were concerned that we should find a good place in the world. To some extent they sacrificed themselves for the sake of the next generation. The message was: if you did as you were told, you would succeed. The practice of religion reinforced the moral code of obedience. It all fitted into what is generally known as a happy childhood.

3

Blairs College

Boyhood ended with a parish mission conducted by the Redemptorist Fathers in 1951. Their hellfire-and-brimstone style of preaching is captured in the school retreat in James Joyce's *A Portrait of the Artist as a Young Man*. However, on this occasion one of the priests had a much gentler approach. He was young, and had a double-barrelled name, Father Lumley-Holmes. One of his tasks was to speak to the top primary class to enquire whether any of the boys were interested in the priesthood. There had been an exhibition about vocations to the religious life in the Kelvin Hall that year – up till then the Hall had been mostly the cavernous venue used at Christmas for the carnival and circus. Three of us put up our hands. I was under the age to be accepted but the other two who volunteered, Charles Corrigan and George McKell, went on to be ordained as Redemptorist priests.

It was a time when young people dreamt of one job for life, whether that was as an engineer or a teacher. There was a definite idea that everyone had a vocation in life. No matter what the work was, the person should do it not just for wages but because it was something that needed to be done. Trying to be a priest or a nun might be more difficult and take a longer training, but it was in a sense a job that any boy or girl might feel called to. There was some glamour around the religious life – *Boys Town* (1938), in which Spencer Tracy played Father Flanagan, was an enduringly popular film; later on, Jennifer Jones had won an Oscar for her role as a visionary and nun in *The Song of Bernadette* (1943). I would not have been identified as 'holier' than the rest of my classmates; it would have just been recognised that I had the ability to give it a good try. There was certainly no persuasion. Our local priests weren't in the business of recruitment, while the teachers were careful not to have favourites. My parents might have been apprehensive, since there was an extra cost involved.

So it was that I received the first letter addressed to me personally: an invitation to attend the entrance exam for Blairs College, Aberdeen, the secondary school for those who applied to join the local diocesan priesthood. The news that I had passed the exam was sent to my parish priest, who was left to tell my parents. Presumably he was to find out what they could contribute to the fees for boarding. My mother went out of her way to say that I should not expect to be treated any differently from my sister or brother. My father, credit to him, was able to say that if I felt it wasn't for me I shouldn't hesitate to return home. It was indeed a bit of a culture shock – I remember on the train to Aberdeen being told by older boys that, 'no, you can't smoke' (I had been helping myself to the occasional cigarette from my father, unknown to him). I also learned it wouldn't be necessary to wear my socks up to knee length, as in public schools.

Day-to-day management of the boys in Blairs was in the hands of the Master of Discipline. At the time I arrived this was a fairly austere character, 'Wally' Crampton. Later it was an eccentric polymath, Danny Boyle, who once chased boys stealing apples from the orchard and claimed to have them 'surrounded'. The rector was the benevolent Steve McGill, later Bishop of Argyll. Father Jack McKee (nicknamed 'The Belloc' because he was constantly quoting the Catholic apologist Hilaire Belloc) taught history in an imperialist British style. I still have a paper I wrote for the history club. The subject was 'Nelson: the English Admiral'; in it, the words English and British are used interchangeably. The other 'profs' made it fairly clear that they were in Blairs under orders from their bishop. One told us so in as many words. Several had studied at Oxford and Cambridge but had not been trained as teachers. Our form master, Father Frank Duffy, was a well-known musician who was keen that his form year put on plays and musicals for the entertainment of the College.

In providing a boarding school for those whom it foresaw would be the 'officers and gentlemen' of the institution, the Catholic Church was aping the wealthier elements of society. In Scotland few boys or girls went to boarding school. They were, in the words of Miss Jean Brodie, the 'crème de la crème'. Blairs followed the classical curriculum of public schools. It also imitated their so-called muscular Christianity. There was little academic ambition. Although it was not oppressively religious, there was a daily programme of devotions from morning Mass to Night Prayer. There was little, if any, room for individual expression of thought. Obedience was top of the list of criteria for progress.

We would return home briefly at Christmas and Easter and had longer summer holidays, when we would meet up with family and friends. Occasionally boys would not return from vacation, having decided the priesthood was not for them. There was a ritual of scoring out their names on the noticeboard and writing RAS, being the Latin *rediit ad suos* ('he has returned to his own'). Names were also scored out for those who left during term-time. They had been 'domied', that is, they had gone home (*domus*), or more likely had been sent home for some infraction of the rules. There were so many rules it seemed relatively easy to be 'shied' (expelled).

My first spiritual notes were on the highly individualistic American Trappist writer Thomas Merton who later said he was 'scandalised by his own Catholicism'. I accepted his, at the time, rather pious account of monastic life. The most popular reading to increase our piety was *The Imitation of Christ* written in the Low Countries by Thomas à Kempis in the fifteenth century. There was no reference to the fact that it was written for adult lay people who were part of the pre-Reformation 'Modern Devotion' movement, which was independent of the clergy. Our hero was St Thérèse of Lisieux, who had got special papal permission to enter a convent at 15 in 1888 and died of TB (tuberculosis) at 24. It was impressed upon us that life was a unique opportunity and we should not presume how much time we had to make the most of it.

I must have been conformist enough, since in my final year I ended up as senior prefect.

In 1956, when the first revolt against Bolshevik Communism took place in Hungary, my mother spoke to us about accepting one of the child refugees who had fled to the West. The family thought this was taking Christian charity a bit too far. At the same time Britain and France briefly invaded Suez to protect their interests in the Canal. I don't remember this being discussed at all. We assumed the British Empire was part of our lives. The new music of Tommy Steele and Glasgow's own Lonnie Donegan were more the subjects of conversation. The social changes this kind of music presaged through Bill Haley and Chuck Berry were not yet on our horizon. We were warned about the dangers of the hip-swivelling Elvis Presley.

Looking back, I have often thought that if you had to go to school, a granite building in ample grounds on the banks of the River Dee wasn't the worst. It had football and cricket pitches and woods to wander in of an afternoon. Many boys, including those who did not become priests, remained life long friends. There was a certain camaraderie among the boys over and against the staff. Psychologists suggest the influence of one's peers may be greater than independent thought or even genes and IQ. It could be reasonably concluded that Blairs left some room for individualism but not for much.

One of the customs at Blairs was that on the last full day of the summer term, at the end of the annual prize-giving, it would be announced where sixth formers, if they were thought suitable, would go for further studies. In our case seven were to report after summer to Cardross, the seminary near Dumbarton, and five to Drygrange in the Borders. Two were to go to Valladolid in Spain and two to San Sulpice in Paris. Five were to make their way to the Scots College in Rome. Those going there were traditionally called out last. Since my name was not among the other destinations I was able to figure out that I was going to Rome. This announcement determined the rest of our education. There was no discussion or questioning. It says a lot about the habit of obedience which had been inculcated in Blairs.

4

Bagarozzi

In 1957 it was a 48-hour journey to Rome – overnight from Scotland, boat train across the Channel and another overnight train journey through Switzerland, being wakened by border guards to show our brand-new passports. The only one amongst us who hadn't been in a junior seminary had lingered in prayer in Westminster Cathedral and missed the boat train, but was able to get the next one from London and catch up with us. He had been joint dux at St Mungo's Academy, Glasgow. We were joined by another who had been at an English seminary. The others had been with me in Blairs. Peter Moran, a future Bishop of Aberdeen, was the senior student deputed to deliver us safely to the Scots College.

When we arrived in Rome the students were at the summer villa at Marino in the Alban Hills. Before joining them, we had to be outfitted with full-length dress-like soutanes, which meant we were immediately identifiable as clerics. We were told this was in case we were tempted to sneak into a café or bar. There was considerable anti-clericalism in Rome. The clergy, including clerical students, were known by the Romans as *bagarozzi*, meaning black beetles. The word came from a Communist poster depicting the clergy as parasites. Our uniform was a purple cassock with a red sash. The only students who were more conspicuous than the Scots were the Germans, whose soutane was a bright red.

In those days the Catholic Church was being compared by the *Reader's Digest* to the American car manufacturer General Motors for its efficiency. The Vatican was the biggest and oldest multinational in the world. However, it was hardly more than a decade since the Second World War, during which the behaviour of the Roman pontiff had been at best perplexing (he helped the Jews in

Rome but not in Germany). Within a year of our arrival, Pius XII died in Castel Gandolfo and we hurried to see him. For some of us it was our first sight of a dead body. His embalming was botched and after we had seen him, his body had to be put into a closed coffin; half a million people passed it in St Peter's before he was buried privately.

We didn't know it at the time, but it was the end of an era.

In his place was elected, to the surprise of many, the 78-year-old Patriarch of Venice, Cardinal Roncalli. As Pope John XXIII, one of his first acts was to announce 23 new cardinals, which took the total above the previously fixed limit of 70. He did a number of other things which were not in the tradition of recent popes – like greeting a Jewish delegation as his brothers. He was not going to be a prisoner in the Vatican like Pius XII, who had jealously protected the independence of the Holy See – which had been guaranteed by the Fascist dictator Mussolini (ironically, this made Pius XII reluctant to act contra the policies of Mussolini and his German ally). He visited Regina Coeli prison at Christmas and in January came to our university, the Gregorianum (known to us 'the Greg'), to the great delight of the students. The Christian Democrats who had ruled Italy since the war announced an *apertura alla Sinistra* (opening to the Left) – but only to the Socialist party, not the Communists.

Pope John tried to start a programme of reform in the Church by holding a synod for the diocese of Rome. The clergy cheerfully agreed to ban the visiting of bars; they then poured out into the streets to enjoy their cappuccinos in the same bars. They agreed not to attend 'spectacles' but later decided this didn't include football matches. The conservative status quo effectively nullified the Pope's attempts at change. It wasn't any better in the Scots College. One of the staff told us that the greatest document in the Church was the 1908 papal encyclical *Pascendi Gregis* (On Feeding the Sheep). This was Pius X's effort to prevent 'Modernism', a movement at the turn of the nineteenth century to try and introduce some liberal thinking into the Catholic Church. In 1958 there was little liberal thinking in Rome.

On 25 January 1959 Pope John stunned the world by announcing an ecumenical council – the first since the Vatican Council of 1869–70 – to determine the role of the Catholic Church in the modern world. Our rector, Philip Flanagan, had previously been rector of the Scots College in Spain and was a self-confessed supporter of Franco. He prepared the Scottish bishops who came for the Second Vatican Council (also commonly known as Vatican II) by advising them to favour a conservative stance. This might not have been difficult, given that Archbishop Campbell of Glasgow told us he said the rosary during the Latin speeches. An Irish bishop was quoted as saying it was a waste of time: 'They talked about nothing except theology.' A bishop from Texas said: 'Are our churches not full?' One of our professors, the Dutch Jesuit Sebastian Tromp, had been used to writing the papal encyclicals without help from more liberal colleagues.

The Greg was a fairly solemn, usually quiet place but one morning, not long after the Second Vatican Council started in 1962, it erupted in a roar. The Curia (the Vatican civil service) had prepared a traditional document on Divine Revelation for discussion. Most Council members had rejected it but without the necessary two-thirds majority. Consequently the Curia intended to go through it line by line. There were students acting as secretaries. The roar at the Greg was in response to a telephone call from one of them to say that the Pope had intervened to remove the document. We later learned this had been under pressure from certain episcopates and their advisors (including a young Father Ratzinger, later Pope Benedict XVI). The roar signalled the beginning of the end of unthinking obedience.

There would now emerge into the open a struggle between the traditionalists and those who were designated progressives. Pope John's intention had been to 'open the windows'. He saw that the 'Barque of Peter' risked being beached while the world moved on. Those who saw the Church as resisting modern trends wanted to defend the values it represented. These were mostly Italians and Spaniards. Opposed to them were bishops from Germany and France, together with those of Belgium and Holland. They had experienced the irrelevance of the Church in the Second World War, when bishops on both sides had blessed their respective bombs. North Americans (though not the Canadians) sided with the traditionalists while the South Americans proved more progressive. The Irish and British bishops appeared to have little to say. Some of them were more Roman than Rome.

Instead of the decree on Divine Revelation, one on the liturgy was introduced because this was thought to be noncontentious. In the 1950s Pius XII had already started the reform of Catholic worship by restoring the Easter Vigil. But the emphasis remained on the ritual rather than the meaning. Amongst ourselves at the Scots College there was disagreement about how we ought to change, with some unwilling to sign a letter to the rector proposing minor changes at the Mass. In the Brazilian College they were opening wide their arms during Mass, while we were told to imagine we had an elastic band restricting them. A newly ordained priest caused amusement because he didn't know which fingers to use when touching the host (wafer) at Benediction. We had taken it upon ourselves to read the tomes on the liturgy by the great German scholar Jungmann. It was quite different from what we saw being done in the College. Gradually what one did – or didn't – do in the liturgy became a test of conformity.

When I started Divinity I bought a Bible. It was the Catholic version by Monsignor Ronald Knox. The spiritual director at the Scots College, Father Matt Kinsella, asked why I had done this. I replied that I intended to read it. He said he thought that wasn't a very good idea, believing it to be 'not a book for the young'. Sedatives and tranquillisers were just coming onto the market at that time. Wee Mattie thought 'purple hearts' were better than the Bible for calming the students' nerves and making them more obedient. Reading the Bible didn't come into his scheme of spiritual development.

I have notes from my time in Rome that speak of the will of the Superior as the will of God. Rules were a revelation of God's will. Christ was obedient and we were called to be 'other Christs'. I wrote that 'if I find myself thinking like a layman I am on the wrong track'. However, I also wrote that I should not confuse the sign with what is being signified: that there is a difference between men and God. Our spiritual director at that time was Tom (later Cardinal) Winning, who told us obedience was more characteristic of the Catholic clergy than celibacy.

For a while I was in charge of providing textbooks for the students. I made an effort to get the latest texts, since the books that had been popular up till Vatican II clearly weren't going to be of much use. In theology we supplemented our studies with books like *The Resurrection* by the French author F.X. Durwell, which opened our minds for the first time to the centrality of Easter. We were restricted by looking at material within the Roman Catholic tradition. *Honest to God* had just been written by the Anglican Bishop John Robinson. The American Harvey Cox's *The Secular City* was about to become a bestseller. During the war the German Evangelical Dietrich Bonhoeffer had spoken of 'religionless Christianity'. The Death of God debate followed. The Jesuit Teilhard de Chardin's posthumously published theory on the evolution of human consciousness, *The Phenomenon of Man*, led to his being disowned by the Vatican. The emphasis in the Greg at the time, even among those who wanted change, was on Catholic orthodoxy. We were offered relatively little scope to explore different ideas.

The thesis I chose to present for my final theological exam in Rome was a study based on the writings of Cardinal John Henry Newman and his relationship with the First Vatican Council (1869–70). Since Newman was brought up as an Anglican, his was not the theology we were being taught, so the choice of subject might have seemed ambitious. I expressed regret that the effect of the Modernist crisis of the 1900s was to limit the influence of Newman in Rome: in the Greg, a Scripture professor gave us references which were all pre-1900.

We should have been studying the arts and sciences instead of learning by rote snippets of medieval philosophy in Latin. A dose of Dante might have done us more good. We were supposed to imbibe 'the mind of the Church' by some kind of osmosis, possibly because we were living next door to its HQ. But the priority seemed to be a conformity to form, rather than individual development. It wasn't entirely the fault of our teachers. Amongst others we had the distinguished English historian of philosophy Frederick Copleston SJ, and a Canadian Jesuit destined to become even more famous, the philosopher Bernard Lonergan. Oddly, we didn't do much Canon Law, which, because Catholic life was determined mostly by the rules of the Church, was a staple of seminaries elsewhere.

A visiting Jesuit gave us *ferverinos*, spiritual pep talks. I noted in my diary: 'Same tripe every time!' He was succeeded by a Scot who was a Vatican astronomer, so at least we learned something about the stars. Generally, our studies felt irrelevant: one senior student, having been told he had passed the final exams, gave away all his books since he believed he wouldn't need them anymore, only to be told he had been appointed to teach in a seminary. It wasn't only the students who felt that what we were being taught was going to be of little use beyond the College – one of the more up-to-date profs at the Greg told us to forget what we had been taught and start again when we got home. People might try to tell us what to do, but they were only trying to prolong a past that had served its purpose.

To get ordained as a priest in the Roman Catholic Church the principal criterion is a promise (not a vow) of obedience to a bishop. In the 1960s there is no doubt that obedience in the sense of conformity to the rules was essential, although that might have been true of most jobs. It was like France during the Nazi administration: after the war everyone claimed to have been in the Resistance. But, as the 1985 documentary about the Holocaust, *Shoah*, revealed, to risk family, job, life, you had to be a non-conformist. And that is rare. Even before the two world wars Freud had said, 'Only very few civilised people are capable of existing without reliance on others or are even capable of coming to an independent opinion. You cannot exaggerate the intensity of people's inner lack of resolution and craving for authority' ('The future prospects of psycho-analytic therapy', 1910). Priests didn't have to be deeply religious. What was expected of them was a good grasp of ritual and a willingness to follow the minutiae of the regulations. This goes some way towards explaining the behaviour of the majority of Catholic clergy during the Second World War, when they did little to aid the Jews.

No matter what one's personal views might be, it was the voice of orthodoxy that was supposed to be heard – and this was not a new approach. The Third Marquess of Bute, who spent a fortune helping restore the Catholic Church in Scotland in the late nineteenth century, regarded the education of the Catholic clergy as problematical. His biographer, Rosemary Hannah, observed in her book *The Grand Designer*: 'There was no concept that a mind exposed to a variety of challenges might become sharper and a faith which was allowed to be tested might grow. Instead the widespread assumption was that any breadth of education would lead to loss of faith. Most priests and bishops wanted a cloistered training which would keep young men from all possible harm' (*The Grand Designer*, p. 317). It was a bit like the Labour Party. Officially it was in favour of the nuclear deterrent. Yet in Scotland many Labour supporters took part in Ban the Bomb marches and protests against the Polaris submarines in the Holy Loch. How did one belong to a party without believing every word it preached?

In war the military had trained men to be ready to go over the top. That, in a figurative sense, is what we thought we were being called to do. No matter what reservations we might have had personally, we were supposed to be ready to defend Roman Catholic assumptions through our promise of obedience to our bishop.

5

Broomhill

There was no shortage of priests for parishes in 1964, the year I graduated. Some of my colleagues were sent to further studies in Cambridge, London, Munich and Rome. I thought I might be among them but I wasn't. There was no question of discussing one's future with superiors. Probably my card had been marked as one of those looking for change in the Church. It was not what the archdiocese of Glasgow was hoping for. There was a tradition of certain priests thought of as too clever not being allowed to do further studies. They were to be kept in their place. It is likely that I was thought to need 'a dose of reality' in a parish. Not that I wasn't looking forward to that; it was what I had been ordained for, and newly established parishes were anxious to get young priests.

I was told to present myself at St Brigid's, Toryglen. It was typical of post-war Glasgow parishes, a housing scheme (estate) in the South Side. It was unusual in that most of the inhabitants seemed to originate from the same part of Donegal. The priest in charge was the larger-than-life Patrick Sheary from Tipperary, whose whole focus seemed to be on paying off in record time the debt incurred from the building of the church. His assistant was a quiet Scot, Jim Cosker, who was the model of obedience. For pastoral practice his rule was 'whatever the Big Man wants'. The Big Man was not God but the parish priest. For the people, Sheary was to all extent and purposes the local pope. It was an invaluable experience of what the Church was like before the Second Vatican Council. I was given a small room and astonished Sheary by asking for a desk. He said he hadn't felt the need to read anything since his time in seminary when he had 'completed' his studies. A parishioner was able to put a folding desk up over the radiator for me. Sheary's priorities were Sunday Mass and fish on Fridays, combating drinking and gambling, promoting Catholic schools and no remarrying after divorce.

Both Sheary and Cosker were dedicated visitors to families. They were always asking me if I had found any new Catholics in the scheme when in fact they would have known if a pigeon had landed. I did find a group of Travelling people once, only for Sheary to tell me a few weeks later that I should be glad to know that 'the bastards' I had brought into 'his' parish had gone!

He might not have been the last of the pre-Vatican II clergy but he was the loudest. His speciality was lengthy sermons at Sunday Mass while Jim Cosker heard confessions. I once timed him at 53 minutes in the pulpit. When I asked him why he talked so long he said it was to allow time for people to go to confession. I told him they were only going to confession for as long as he was talking!

After Father Sheary's death many years later I was invited back for the fortieth anniversary of St Brigid's primary school. It was a sad moment, for his name was not mentioned. The attitude of the people had changed, if not that of the clergy. They did what they were told at the time, but many grew up to resent his domineering behaviour. Nowadays it would be described as bullying. The haemorrhaging of church attendance is as much due to that kind of attitude as to anything else. Not surprisingly, parishioners wanted to retaliate against the bad treatment they or their relatives had received. Religious practice had been reduced to 'duties', like attending Ash Wednesday and Good Friday. In a similar way, the faith of Abraham in Genesis had been reduced to obeying the commandments of Moses in Deuteronomy.

Shortly after Christmas 1964 I was summoned by the archbishop and told I was to start at Glasgow University after summer. I asked if I could commute from Toryglen and was assured that would be no problem, but the following week I got a letter telling me to pack my bags and report within the week to a parish nearer the university. In those days parish priests got ten days to organise themselves when they were transferring to another charge but assistant priests were given only three days, possibly to deprive them of the opportunity to say anything about it from the pulpit on the Sunday. It says a lot for the efficiency if not for the humanity of the system. Parish priests, unlike their assistants, have legal tenure. Despite the idea of 'blind obedience', they cannot be moved against their will. In my time three Galloway priests appealed successfully to Rome to prevent their bishop from moving them. Parish priests might complain about being moved, but they usually accept a new appointment if they are hoping for promotion. Back then, it didn't occur to junior priests – as I then was – to question a move. At that time one might as well have been a bit of furniture being repositioned. No doubt other minions in large organisations have a similar experience.

My new parish priest, Pat Smith, surprised me by saying that as I had just come from Rome I would know how to put into practice the liturgical changes. The new church in Broomhill had been designed by Charles Gray with the revised liturgy in mind. At its opening the preacher described the building as 'the first fruit of Vatican II'. It is difficult to overestimate the effect of these changes to Catholics whose main contact with the Church was on Sundays. Latin in the Mass was replaced by English, the priest faced the people instead of having his back to them and the chalice was to be made available to all. It was all done by diktat, and was a great demonstration of Catholic discipline. Many were unsure or unhappy, but eventually all had to conform.

The phrase 'the Liturgical Movement' came into use. The authorities didn't think it was a blueprint for a new kind of Church because it had not occurred to them that a new Church might be needed. Younger priests thought, naively, that education could be combined with worship. I wrote to Bishop Thompson of Motherwell after he said it was 'not yet opportune' to restore the sign of peace during Mass. He replied perceptively saying that parishes were not genuine communities. In 1966 there was an instruction about the liturgy which kept the Canon of the Mass (the words of consecration) in Latin, with the sharing of the chalice with the laity reserved for special occasions. It took four more years for the Mass to be celebrated entirely in English. Some, among the congregations as well as within the clergy, saw Latin as part of an imagined Golden Age of the Church. Their resulting ignorance of the significance of Church dates and rituals was starkly obvious when, on the First Sunday of Advent, the beginning of the Church's calendar, I wished the congregation a happy new year. They were bemused. Similarly, there was clearly a need for the campaign to 'put Christ back into Christmas'. The truth went deeper – we needed to put Christ back into Christians. Changes in Sunday worship could in essence be traced back to the Reformation and had long been hoped for by some Catholics. Proposals long denied were enacted. Dogmatic questions long avoided were addressed. Disciplinary issues long suppressed were faced. However, they required other, deeper changes in the Church which were not acted upon. The new access to regular communion should have signalled a democratisation of the Church. What was needed was the initiation of lay responsibility. This was ducked. There were by that time many educated and able Catholics, but they were regarded as being too independent-minded and therefore not to be trusted in the same way as compliant clergy.

The staff of the local seminary were apparently divided on how to proceed. The archbishop fired half of them, later saying he did not know whether he had fired the guilty half or not. For him, religion was social rather than prophetic. There was a lay-led Renewal Movement which invited eminent speakers to Glasgow. When they invited the archbishop to a lecture by the radical German Father Hans Kung, he wrote back to say he regarded the invitation as an impertinence. The local Catholic newspaper wanted to run a series on the 'progressive' Dutch Church, but this was blocked by the protests of parish priests. In truth the changes in the Church were a response to the signs of the times. I appreciated people had different views about these changes but I was less than sympathetic to them. The words of Vatican II became the New Law, to which I conformed.

I had been told to study Classics (Greek and Latin) at university but after two years I was bored rigid. Someone had written in my second-hand textbook the old doggerel: 'Greek is a language as dead as dead can be. It killed the ancient Greeks and now it's killing me.' In Glasgow University's Classics department Latin was a study of pre-Christian sources with the sixteenth-century Scottish humanist George Buchanan as exemplar; it held no interest for me. For relief I had also taken a class in the Principles of Religion. I was encouraged to read Martin Buber, the Austrian-Jewish existentialist who had become popular among religious groups by distinguishing between I-Thou and I-It relationships. I met the professor of divinity, the Bultmann scholar Gregor Smith. 'You do know,' he said to me, 'the bones of Jesus are in Palestine?' This was typical of the discussion taking place in Reformed circles, but not in the Roman Catholic Church, as to whether Jesus rose again after death. These were ideas about the origins and meaning of faith that I had not been previously exposed to.

I had also taken a class in psychology. This gave me a choice of subjects to pursue at honours level. When I asked the archbishop, James Scanlan, if I could change to psychology his only comment was that I was not to blame him if I lost my faith as a result. I thought his answer was a greater challenge to faith than anything the psychologists might have to say about religion. One of the lecturers played the organ at an Episcopal church but the professor of psychology Ralph Pickford was a genuine Freudian – and Freud was considered one of the threats to organised religion .

I was at university in 1968, when students everywhere were protesting, not just those led by 'Red' Rudi Dutschke in Berlin and Daniel Cohn-Bendit in Paris. It was the time of Flower Power in the USA. Anti-authoritarianism was in full swing. The film *If* . . . suggested boarding schools were to blame for revolt. Czechoslovakia was invaded by the Soviets. The PLO was formed. There was Woodstock and a choice between the Beatles and the Rolling Stones. The Americans made another 'final effort' in Vietnam. Martin Luther King and Robert Kennedy were assassinated. Cassius Clay became Muhammad Ali. In Glasgow University the graffiti in the lecture rooms became political.

When I finished my degree Scanlan told me I had studied enough and it was time to return to parish work. I guessed the archdiocese thought psychology was not a useful qualification. I tried to explain to him that the degree in itself was not sufficient, and I had been offered a place for professional training. He said to me: 'You don't understand. You only have to be obedient. I have the task of telling people what to do!' It was a massive insight into the system. It wasn't, as I had thought, about obedience to the Gospel: it was about playing one's part in a great game. The archbishop could have been described as the last of the prince bishops. You might have imagined him being downed from his horse by an arrow in Kelvingrove Park. He was uncharitably described as never having let religion interfere with his career.

Some of the staff at university were disappointed that I was not going on to take the professional qualification in psychology and appealed to him. Embarrassed by their approach, he reconsidered his decision and allowed me to further my studies – but in a different parish. The appearance of obedience had to be maintained. I had thought I was being obedient – I had accepted his prerogative. It is not how others saw me. The fact that I had even tried to argue with the archbishop might have indicated that I wanted my own way. A crisis of obedience was emerging in me between the dictates of authority and freedom of conscience.

6

Bridgeton

After graduating in psychology in 1969 there were a number of branches of the discipline one could choose to be trained in. Clinical psychology might have frightened the Church authorities too much so I opted for educational psychology. The first year for the diploma at that time in Scotland meant qualifying as a teacher. The style at Jordanhill Training College for Teachers was fairly conventional. One student was ordered out of the lecture room for bringing in a cup of coffee. I got the chance to work my way through training experiences at different levels. My first term placement was in Shettleston Nursery, where I sat among the tiny tots. After Christmas I went to St Michael's School for primary training. This was, conveniently, next door to where I was living. I completed the year at St Mary's Junior Secondary, which had once been in Calton but had been transferred to bigger premises in an old non-denominational building in Bridgeton.

The second year of the educational psychology course was back at university. I moved on to training in child guidance. As part of the course I got a place with Dr Isobel Sutherland at the Child Psychiatry Unit. I was given the case of a badly behaved girl who had severe visual problems. I was asked to investigate which caused which: was her eyesight the reason for her poor behaviour or not? It gave me the chance to get my teeth into a real practical problem and the Psychiatry Unit was pleased with my report. All 24 of us who had started out graduated as educational psychologists. At the end of the course there proved to be jobs on offer for everyone in the local authorities.

Geoffrey Dell, principal psychologist for the city, agreed there was a place for a psychologist dedicated to St Mary's, the last junior secondary school in the city, which had a fair proportion of the local child guidance clinic's cases. The boys and girls came from nine primaries spread over the East End. They tended to truant – and if they weren't going to school, they were even less likely to attend a clinic. I had already been given permission by the archdiocese to spend part of the day in the school. Bridgeton senior psychologist Ian Macdonald was receptive to the idea of my working there as school psychologist. The head teacher, Amato Renucci, welcomed the appointment. He had been a pioneer in the teaching of maths to less able pupils.

St Mary's was understaffed, even though some of the older male teachers boasted of having been able to run a card school all day in the past (alleging there were always teachers free to conduct a game of cards, albeit in a rota). School standards were dictated by the expectations of parents. The expectations at a 'junior' secondary were low. There were two excellent 'senior' secondaries beside us, one for girls run by Franciscan Sisters and the other for boys by Marist Brothers. The climax of indiscipline in St Mary's came when a temporary music teacher was hit by her own bassoon. Enough was enough. It was decided not to accept any more teachers who were unaware of the school's special needs. Gradually new young teachers volunteered and the ethos changed.

The pupils at St Mary's had what the psychologist John Rutter called 'a precocious level of psycho-social independence'. At home the parents were often unable either physically or mentally to supervise their families. This kind of independence was seldom an asset when it came to dealing with the harsh realities of working in the world. The corollary of obedience is discipline. Without discipline in the home the young person is going to be shocked by how much it is needed in further education or at work.

My course dissertation had been on the Swiss psychologist Jean Piaget and his ideas on the formation of conceptual thinking in children. I sought to apply this to the teaching of the catechism in Catholic schools. I had the opportunity to examine all of the first-year pupils in St Mary's junior secondary school with respect to their level of religious understanding. The progressive Irish monthly, *The Furrow*, published my results with the heading 'Too much too soon'. I concluded that 'there is no such thing as a specifically religious way of thinking' and 'worship is not intelligible in non-communal terms'.

By the summer of 1969 I had been appointed as one of four priests in St Michael's, Parkhead, so was working at St Mary's alongside this. The parish priest told me I would have no time to work as a psychologist. His profile was etched in sweat on his armchair – he clearly spent a lot of time in it – so I reckoned I would be able to manage two jobs. One of the assistant priests, jolted by my arrival, decided to join the British Army as a chaplain. Rather incredibly the other assistant, Father Bartie Burns, was being followed by the Special Branch because it was suspected he was associating with the IRA – he knew he was being followed, but I only found out later. The new church, which was opened shortly after I arrived, seated 800. Out of a possible roll of 4,000 parishioners it was estimated that about 1,000 went to the five Sunday Mass times that were on offer.

A new parish priest, Micky Lyne, was brought into St Michael's to deal with the debt incurred by the new church. He had been a promising Gaelic footballer in his day. He played the game during his summer holidays in Ireland despite having been forbidden by the Church. I reminded him of this when he was wont to lecture me on obedience. As a curate he had climbed onto a roof to talk a man down and got his ankle sliced by a slate thrown at him. Despite this he went to Celtic Park every weekday to train. His day was passed in a frantic round of school, hospital and home visiting. He would watch the first few minutes of *News at Ten* before disappearing to bed with a bag of sweets and the evening paper. He had no interest in Vatican II and it was said he would baptise anything that moved. Despite our differences we got on well, probably because his focus was on the parish and encouraging devotions while I was working equally hard at other things – he disapproved of complacency, once describing a certain priest as too lazy to go to the toilet. Because he affected such a macho exterior, when he was promoted to the rank of Canon he arranged to have his photo in his new robes taken secretly.

There were two contrasting factions trying to effect change in the Church in Scotland after Vatican II. One worked through the diocesan Council of Priests. This was managed mostly by older clergy who wanted minimum change. The other was among the many younger priests who would get together to debate theology rather than play golf or cards. I joined a group in Lanarkshire called the Clonmacnoise (after the great Irish monastic centre of learn-ing), which met regularly. We discussed, for example, how the Bishop of Motherwell, an able fellow, could confess in public that he had not yet read all the Vatican documents. As long as priests did what they were told, he believed, the organisation would be in good health. Two of his priests, friends of mine, disagreed with his slow pace of change. He was happy to let them go to other dioceses.

I had by this time acquired some self-awareness. Curiosity was my main driving force in exploring fields that priests would not have thought open to them. It was said St Augustine was against '*curiositas*' because it was a consequence of Original Sin. I had become cynical about authority because it was clearly unwilling and/or unable to manage the changes I saw as necessary to bring the Church into the modern world. My friends told me I was inclined to act in a boorish fashion and indulge in sarcasm. The truth was I had come to dislike being stereotyped as a cleric. In the circles I moved in there was an assumption that priests were poorly educated. I had, on the other hand, become quite sure of myself – for better and for worse. I didn't think the education the rest of society had received was all that better than mine. I was described as being judgemental – not just about religious opinions but about anything I didn't agree with. I hadn't been tested to the point of disobedience but I was becoming used to getting my own way. I had got beyond the stage of conforming to the expectations of others.

7

Bangladesh

The Church of Scotland minister in Parkhead, Frank Grimes, gave an interesting slant on the difference between obedience and servility. During the Second World War he had been in the army in India. He had asked the Indian servant one day if it was going to rain. The servant asked: 'Do you like rain, sahib?' Frank's response would determine the answer. This was in Jessore, which was now in Bangladesh. Jessore was to be my next destination.

I had always had in mind that I would work in Glasgow for the first 10 years of my priesthood – to pay back, as it were, what had been invested in my education. After that I would feel free to try to explore the wider world. The idea of freedom, and being free to do something, was important for me. In the summer of 1975 I went on retreat to a religious house at Massingham in Norfolk. It was attended by young priests and nuns seeking how best to develop their vocation. While there, I wrote down some thoughts based on the text, 'the truth shall make you free' (John 8:32): 'Freedom is the most precious gift. Free, that is, to be oneself. Christ is the way, the truth and the life for me. We live in an age of further revelation of Incarnation and the transformation of symbols away from special or sacred times, places and people towards ordinary and secular experience. On this basis I choose to exercise my freedom.'

Although Glasgow had many priests, few had volunteered to work overseas. My friends joked that when I asked Archbishop Scanlan for permission he had said 'Yes, please!' This was not exactly true. His auxiliary bishop, Tom Winning, helped to get me permission to go away. Then Scanlan resigned suddenly. Unexpectedly, Winning was appointed in his place. He asked me to change my mind. He wanted me to succeed the charismatic Gerry Hughes SJ as the chaplain at the University of Glasgow.

Gerry had constantly been in conflict with the authorities. I had no intention of putting myself into such a situation. Moreover, I did not feel any call to work with students. I arranged instead to become an affiliate of the Italian Xaverian Fathers, whom I knew from their house in Glasgow. Curiously, the Confirmation name I had chosen as a child was St Francis Xavier. One of their missions in Bangladesh was a training centre in Jessore for local catechists, and they thought the Centre could benefit from someone who was an English speaker and was qualified in educational methods.

I went to Bangladesh aged 35, in the prime of my life, having signed up to stay for five years. It was the loneliest thing I had ever done, and at a time when things at home were changing at last. My work as a psychologist in Bridgeton had been given recognition, and educational opportunities were opening up. Archbishop Winning was about to introduce Vatican II programmes into the Church in Glasgow. My parents were both in their 70s: with travel limited at the time it was possible, even likely, I might not see them again. My youngest nieces had just started school. I would not see the older ones in their teenage years. I would also be leaving behind close friends, one of whom had given me a tear-stained Bible to take with me.

Before I left, on the last day of a holiday in Ireland, I woke up to the news that there had been a coup in Bangladesh. Government ministers had been killed and the military had taken over. Kissinger had described the country as a 'basket case'. *The Economist* was writing that Bangladesh could be the first modern country to cease to exist. A month later, the Air India plane I took to Dhaka was mostly empty. It was the first to fly in since the coup. The priest detailed to meet me didn't turn up because he got the chance to change some money at a favourable rate elsewhere.

There was an Englishman in the airport who saw me looking lost. He advised me to take a taxi to the convent of the American Holy Cross Sisters, who were surprised to find a Scotsman on their doorstep. They sent me to the bishop's house, where some of the Italian Xaverians were on retreat. I was put on a local flight to Jessore, in the south-west of the country, where Father Lucio Ceci collected me on a Vespa. He delivered me to the Catholic hospital, where Xaverian Brother Dr Renato Bucari knew friends of mine in Glasgow. There was just one person from Britain, a nurse, Angela King, from Sunderland.

What I had to do first, much to my surprise, was to learn the local language. The Bangladeshi bishops had agreed that all new personnel coming to the country would have to learn Bengali. I had no sooner arrived than I was whisked down south to language school. It was a test of obedience to a bishop I hadn't even met. There can hardly be a truer examination of character than settling down to learn a language as an adult. One becomes again a child. In retrospect it was the best possible start. I was reduced to silence, only gradually being enabled to talk again. I spent a full year in listening mode. Bengali is the sixth biggest language group in the world. On the sub-continent Bangladesh was unusual in that most people spoke the one language; its expressiveness is reflected in the work of Bengali poet and writer Rabindranath Tagore, who won the Nobel Prize for Literature in 1913.

The Language Institute was run by a large French Canadian, Père Tourangeau. After Vatican II, most of the French Canadian priests in Bangladesh had returned to Canada. They believed it was time for local people to take over. His deputy was Father Georges LaPrade, who seemed to be made of steel. He slept outside on a wicker mat. He told us that once, while off the beaten track, he had taken ill. The locals recommended that he swallow some snake venom as a cure. This he had done, and he survived. Some of the Italians were also very ascetic. I visited Padre Corba in his hermitage in the north. I had to push my bike the last couple of miles when the road ran out. He had a little tortoise in a bucket of water, which I thought quite touching till it appeared on the table for our dinner.

Bangladesh is a beautiful country sitting on the Gangetic Delta. The different seasons give it three rice harvests per year. As a 'Britisher' I received respect. Many looked back wistfully at 'Rajer Somoy' (the time of the Raj), when everyone was treated the same – i.e. rich and poor were disciplined alike by the colonial power. They also remembered the Scots who worked for the Bengal Inland Transport and Waterways Authority. They wanted to know what language they used when they spoke to each other! Some of the older American missionaries remembered the Great Bengal Famine of 1943, when no rice was available in the markets because it was being stored to sell to the British Army, which was preparing to launch the invasion into Burma from India.

At Partition in 1947 the great Indian states of Punjab and Bengal were divided along religious lines. In eastern India the Hindu part became West Bengal and the Muslim part became East Pakistan, 1,000 miles from its other half, West Pakistan. There was constant political agitation in East Pakistan for more autonomy from West Pakistan, and in 1971 the Pakistan election gave power to the more populous East. However, the army arrested the Eastern leaders and held them in Islamabad in West Pakistan, and then tried to enforce the Muslim version of Hindi (Urdu) on East Pakistan (where they spoke Bengali); revolt ensued. Indian intervention brought it quickly to an end. At the ceasefire apparently the respective generals proposed a cricket match between the two sides, but Mrs Ghandi put a stop to that. As so often happens after revolution, the rebels failed to agree with each other and there was a coup. The founding father of Bangladeshi independence, Sheikh Mujibur Rahman, was assassinated and government ministers massacred. The commanding officer of the new Bangladesh Army, Colonel Zia, took over. The military remained in charge for all of my time in the country.

On the waterways, which had been the most common form of travel in Bengal, I saw a boat whose engines had been made in Denny's of Dumbarton in 1929. Meanwhile Toyota buses just imported from Japan were lying with their engines burned out on the single-track roads. There is a saying that neo-colonial states produce what they don't consume and consume what they don't produce. This was the problem Bangladesh faced in trying to modernise itself. Was being exploited better than not being traded with at all?

Before my arrival some of the missionaries had been involved in the 'aid business'. The Xaverians had recently had a priest killed by robbers who were looking for aid money and another had been shot dead in the 1971 War of Independence. During my time there was much debate among the priests about a new kind of colonialism that was powered by aid from overseas. Any kind of welfare work clearly saved lives. Could the poor afford to wait until their own country could develop sufficiently to provide for their needs?

In terms of law and order it would have to be said that the country fulfilled the criteria to be a 'functioning anarchy', as described by Gunnar Myrdal in his 1968 book *Asian Drama: An Inquiry into the Poverty of Nations*. The weakness of the new governments after independence permitted corruption rather than mere conformity. Those who had conformed enough to be servants in colonial days became the new masters without the restraints of imperial laws. Many of the Italian priests were on the left politically. My colleague Father Ceci was a Marxist who disappeared from time to time to meet up with the families of the left-wing Naxalite rebel group. Those who were working in the training centre had their own ideas of what they wanted to teach. The Xaverians had a great saying: *C'è posto per tutti* – there's room for everybody. The Italians spoke Bengali well and presumed they would be in Bangladesh for the rest of their lives. It was an excellent example of dedication.

The Christians in Bangladesh were of three classes. A small number around the capital were connected to old Anglo-Indians, although with the names of the Portuguese who had converted them. The second group were not Bengalis but Adibashi, the aboriginal or tribal inhabitants of the border hills who had become Christian more recently. Their land was often disputed by Muslim incomers. The rest of the Christians were among the poorest class. They had been outcasts, 'untouchables', and not even the Muslims wanted them. However, by getting a mission education and better healthcare they had climbed the social ladder. Our mission hospital was preferred by everyone in the local area. Brother Bucari insisted on a small fee from everyone, even the Christians, somewhat to their chagrin.

Father Bill McIntyre, who had travelled widely, was the Superior of five Maryknoll missionaries who had just been sent from the United States to Bangladesh. He told me that the Catholic Church in Bangladesh was very conservative. As if to confirm this, the religious books for the diocese of Khulna, to which I now belonged, were brought from Calcutta, across the border in Bengali-speaking India. The bishops were shocked, too, when an Indian Jesuit expert they had invited said he would only come if the priests cancelled Sunday Mass to spend a week with him. In their meetings they debated why they were not being persecuted by the government, as was happening in other developing, or as we called them then, Third World countries. We were not outspoken enough, they concluded.

The Muslims at that time were conservative rather than fundamentalist. The money for their Madrasa schools had begun to come as aid from Saudi Arabia, but the revival of political Islam had not yet taken place. There was no hint of the violence that was to come later. There was a saying: 'The further from Mecca, the further from Allah'. It was understood, however, that no Muslim could become Christian. The Archbishop of Dhaka put it succinctly: 'If you foreigners annoy the government you will be sent home; we Bengalis will be put in prison or killed.'

The military government was fond of urging the local people to 'work as hard as the missionaries'. But we weren't allowed to describe ourselves as missionaries. Most of the Italian priests had other qualifications which enabled them to operate in development projects. The Sisters ran the schools while the Brothers had engineering workshops. My qualification as a psychologist had been enough to get me into the country. When I had applied for an entry visa I had got it the next day. The official in the embassy expressed surprise that I would want to work in Bangladesh.

Religious discrimination by the Muslims was directed at the remaining Hindus – still almost 15 per cent of the population. They had been the great landowners in Bengal. At Partition most had fled across to the Indian side. I was interested in the local culture, which was still heavily influenced by Hinduism. I wanted an introduction to the elements of yoga. In Jessore there was a Muslim who was able to teach it. He showed me the physical moves but was uninterested in any spiritual explanation.

Thousands of men were bussed into the local football stadium for the main Muslim feasts. Cultural conformity might explain part of this religious practice. The Christians faced the criticism of having inherited their status from the patronage of the former imperial power, even though there had been Christians in the Indian sub-continent before the arrival of Islam. Christians were seen as owing obedience to foreign powers.

8

Barlinnie before the Riot

By 1980, the year I returned to Scotland, Mrs Thatcher had been Prime Minister in Britain for a year. Khomeini had taken over in Iran. Bob Dylan was telling us that nobody was free. After five years overseas I had a dilemma. On the one hand I had learned, not without cost, the Bengali language. I enjoyed the work in the training centre and got on well with the Italian missionaries. On the other hand I did believe that some of the problems hindering the development of Bangladesh could be traced back to Western control of the global economy. It was the British Raj that had introduced capitalism into India when it was a rural economy. Bangladesh in large part still depended on village enterprises. But Westernisation was clearly coming. It made some sense to return and, fortified by my own experience, to try to convince others that we had to change our own attitudes. I hoped the totally different experience of living in a country like Bangladesh would give me the courage to speak up where others might hesitate.

A couple of years after my return, by now aged 42, I was invited to become a chaplain at Barlinnie Prison, Glasgow, Scotland's largest jail. Barlinnie was dirtier than Bangladesh and worse for the health of its inhabitants. At least in Bangladesh the people got some chance to look after themselves. In Barlinnie men were held two to a cell. They had no say about whom they would be locked up with. It could have been a murderer or someone with mental health problems. Access to the toilet was strictly controlled and each prisoner had a chamber pot for use in the cell. A shower once a week with a change of underwear was grudged by the staff. As Pirsig said in *Zen and the Art of Motorcycle Maintenance*, the prison officers 'were involved but not in such a way as to care'. The prison demonstrated what has been called the great coalition between habit and lethargy.

The previous Catholic chaplain had been a special constable with little sympathy for prisoners. The archbishop discussed with me the idea of sending several younger priests to share responsibilities in the prison. It would be their job to change the impression that the Church was simply going along with the system. I suspected it might suit the non-conformist part of my own nature to volunteer. My mother was disappointed but my father was pleased. He recalled he had been asked to play the organ at a service in Barlinnie and had got into an argument with an officer for defending Mary, Queen of Scots.

To say the prison authorities were surprised by the arrival of three younger priests would be an understatement. The chief warder said that although he was a different religion he would try and help us. I asked if he was Hindu. He said he was a Baptist. I assured him he was of the same religion as us. He relaxed enough to say that he drove a horse and cart for recreation. Father John McGinley agreed to take the lead. He would later become principal psychologist at the state prison at Carstairs. Father Larry McMahon, a hail-fellow-well-met type, took care of the Special Unit. It was the focus of much media attention for its pioneering work with Jimmy Boyle and other awkward characters. My responsibility was to be the remand wing. This was a large proportion of the prison population, crammed into one hall.

There was still belief in the 'short, sharp shock'. No research existed to say whether this worked or not. My first impression was that those who didn't obey the rules were held hostage, as it were, *pour encourager les autres*. In other words, they were there to make sure that others in similar positions behaved. It was believed there was a criminal sub-class who would never change. They had to be restrained as much as possible. The truth was that the majority were fairly feckless characters who, as the governor told us at our initiation process, happened to be in the wrong place at the wrong time.

Although remand prisoners were legally innocent, their conditions were worse than for the convicted. This was because they were held for a relatively short time. For minor charges they could be imprisoned for a few days or a couple of weeks at most. The longest anyone could be held in remand in Scotland was 110 days. The prison was unwilling to waste money on remand prisoners by providing decent facilities for them. I was always easily offended by establishment attitudes. The staff knew the conditions remand prisoners were being kept in but did nothing about it. At a meeting with the governors I suddenly put on the table a pillow I had taken from a cell. This was not too easy to procure as the prisoners didn't want to create trouble. The governors jumped. It was alive with lice.

People had no idea what went on behind prison doors. Many thought criminals got what they deserved. There was an opinion that having to obey the rules in prison would teach prisoners a lesson. This attitude was reflected in a 1990 STV series on the legal system presented by Kirsty Young; the pilot programme was with a group of mothers of murdered children who, like the majority of the population, thought prison was too soft on the convicted. I was able to describe how bad Barlinnie was. The truth was, many inmates had never learned respect for social conventions. They regarded prisons as the ultimate in hypocrisy, because they experienced the justice system as based on class, with the better-off judging the less well-off. The poor had no lawyers of their own who could keep them out of jail.

One of the first prisoners I met, Frank, a young man in his twenties with special needs, had jumped into the canal to get attention from his mother. He was jailed for breach of the peace. In prison he got a kicking from the officers for ringing the bell for help. Another, Robert, also had special needs. He was being punished for petty theft and being a pest to society. I took both of them home. Frank never returned to prison. Robert gradually worked himself up to a 10-year sentence for repeatedly stealing small sums of money. Judges, although they had been to school like the rest of us, thought if a punishment didn't work the first time, then doubling it might do the trick. Inmates began to recognise me outside on the streets where they continued to panhandle, having learned nothing from their time inside – there was very little in the way of education in the prison, and the experience itself made no impression. They regarded their punishment as a hazard of living where they did.

The prison required us to provide a religious service each Sunday. We managed to persuade the staff to sit at the back instead of on high chairs around the hall. Some prisoners came for the devotion, some for the break and others to meet their pals. We invited various groups to come and provide music. The Catholic chaplains were also expected to offer the sacrament of confession to the prisoners. On one occasion a prisoner wrote 'send for Beltrami' over the notice saying where confessions would be held – he was a Glasgow lawyer famous for getting criminals out of being convicted.

One Easter Sunday we gave out chocolate eggs after Mass. Some of the longer-term prisoners waited till the end, hoping to get extra. When we ran out of eggs we had to skip smartly down to the shops for more. These serious criminals were counting on getting their chocolate egg.

One year, going against the public perception of civil servants as being intellectually lazy and cautious, Her Majesty's Inspector of Prisons criticised prison chaplains at the General Assembly of the Church of Scotland in Edinburgh. He thought we should be speaking out more about the conditions. He expected chaplains to be more supportive of him because we witnessed what was going on.

As prison chaplains, we were bound by the Official Secrets Act. This was meant to prevent anyone outside finding out what was going on inside. For me it meant, rather, taking the consequences if you decided to become a whistleblower. The touchpaper proved to be a directive which I happened to catch sight of about the transfer of prisoners, including 'problem' ones, to other jails. Being transferred suddenly to another prison often caused trouble because it interfered with visits. It was difficult, if not impossible, for some relatives or friends to get to a distant prison. I remembered being told in an American prison that the main ways to keep the peace were to provide good food and not interfere with visits. At our chaplains' meetings at Barlinnie at that time we all felt that the place had reached boiling point, so at the next meeting with Church of Scotland colleagues I said I thought that major trouble was brewing there. My remarks were reported to the Scottish Office in Edinburgh, which relayed them to the Prison Department.

The upshot was that I was sent for by the Barlinnie governor. He was nicknamed 'Slasher' because he had once offered to take on a prisoner in a 'square go' (fight). He said he was going to fire me for criticising his prison. I told him I had been appointed by Archbishop Winning: he would have to phone him. Winning already had a social-justice reputation – there was no way a governor was going to tell him he was dismissing one of his priests. The archbishop would, to say the least, be put out by the suggestion that any of his priests were not good enough. When I told him what was happening, he stood by me. The institution which sent me to the prison was strong enough to support me when I felt obliged to support the Inspector of Prisons. It was a modest contribution; there was a terrible atmosphere in Barlinnie at that time, and the ferment was building up. In terms of obedience, however, I had discovered that a command structure could be useful.

9

Barlinnie after the Riot

In January 1987 the roof literally came off Barlinnie. A group of prisoners made their way onto it and in full view of the world's media broke up the tiles. There had already been riots in several prisons in England. It was the effect of social changes which had not been recognised by the prison establishment. Old lags just accepted the appalling conditions of the prisons, but the younger prisoners wouldn't. When I pointed out that in the 1980s young men were used to regular showers, and said that prisoners should be able to use the phone, the officers laughed. Innocent family visitors were treated as if they too were criminals. Even medicine in the remand hall was restricted to paracetamol, handed out from a drawer in proportion to the complaint.

The riot was only ended by the intervention of the 'Papal Guard', a group of officers trained to deal with any trouble – so-called because they were led by a prominent Catholic. The prisoners agreed to come down if a Catholic chaplain was on hand to make sure they didn't get a kicking. After the riot the governor, who had called for the reintroduction of manacles, was moved sideways. Later he got a gong. The prisoner who led the riot got 12 years. The governor should have got the jail and the prisoner the medal.

It had been the perception of the prisoners that the staff did nothing except open and close cell doors when required to. The officers now got new training and began to work for the betterment of the prisoners. Previously the officers had only been required to be stronger than the prisoners. Now they wanted to be generally fitter. They were given the opportunity to acquire new qualifications. Up till then the police, and even more so prison staff (and there was no love lost between the two services), had been recruited from a level in society that had low aspirations. With better training and more support, more able candidates were now beginning to apply to join the prison service. One of the new governors appointed, Andrew Coyle, had been a priest. He went on to lead the Scottish Prison Service in a root-and-branch reform.

At the time of the riot I had completed five years as a prison chaplain. It was understood that chaplains would stay on for 10 years. Our work offered continuity after the riot. Our potential to help in rehabilitation was recognised. In those days, most of the inmates smoked – one of their few comforts – so I set up a cigarette fund for the unconvicted (remand) prisoners, some of whom had no visitors to help them out financially. Only the convicted were entitled to a small wage for work. I also worked ecumenically to establish a chaplaincy board which eventually created two full-time posts at the Scottish Prison Service headquarters for a Church of Scotland minister and a Catholic priest.

Barlinnie was a drying-out place for those seriously affected by booze. The rich seldom committed crime under the influence of alcohol. The poor did. The police routinely picked up those under the influence of drink and processed them through the courts. Even the murders were often alcohol related. This radically questioned the purpose of prison. Imprisonment depends entirely on obedience. Or rather conformity. The prisoners were required to obey the rules, but for most of them their minds were elsewhere. For some it was on their first drink when they got out. There was an early pub opening for the morning workers at Blochairn Fruit Market, which was not far from the prison. This is where they used to head for, and the cycle of reoffending would begin again almost immediately. An Alcoholics Anonymous group visited the prison, but despite the improvements in recruitment and training, they didn't get much support from staff.

★★★

While I was at Barlinnie, I took the opportunity to visit the other prisons in Scotland. Most prisoners were being kept in Dickensian conditions. For the size of the country, Scotland has a relatively large prison population, one of the largest in Europe. The main idea in most of the places seemed to be retribution rather than rehabilitation. This was the case even in the Young Offenders Institution at Polmont. Women were all held centrally at Cornton Vale near Stirling, which didn't help visiting from other parts of the country. The press had published concerns that women prisoners were over-medicated.

I also went to see the prison systems in other countries, visiting several in England. In my time Scottish prisons had no prisoners of a different ethnic background to speak of. In England that wasn't the case. There was no special provision for them and they met in prison the same discrimination as outside. The English prisons also held mafia types, and with this combination were therefore more difficult to manage. During 'the Troubles' they also held IRA prisoners. I visited Mountjoy Prison in Dublin and saw the memorial to Kevin Barry, who had been executed there. The staff seemed unsure whether he was a martyr or a criminal.

In the United States I met a prisoner halfway through the second of his three 25-year sentences. A jail I saw in Hong Kong was run like a Chinese laundry – busy all the time – much to the distress of foreign nationals, who were mostly hippies in for drug offences. In Ghana a prisoner was made to carry the security gun, since it was beneath the dignity of the officer to do so (it wouldn't have occurred to the poor prisoner to use it – I couldn't have believed it if I hadn't seen it).

Throughout my travels to visit prisons elsewhere, I was struck by the enormous differences among countries that were often lumped together by academics as 'underdeveloped'. Much of South America, for example, was governed by military regimes which were strong on law and order. In several of them popular movements for change were beginning to appear. Revolution happens when there is hope of change, but protestors, when they were not killed, were imprisoned in large numbers. I visited Father Frank Kennedy, who had been a shipyard chaplain on Clydeside and had gone to Argentina as a one-man peace mission after the Falklands/ Malvinas debacle. Ironically, having become a parish priest there, he found himself having to preach in the local military academy.

Africa was quite different. The tight structures of organised religions like Christianity, Hinduism, Buddhism or Islam were lacking. There was anarchy. The leaders of the major tribes had collaborated with the colonial authorities in order to effect a transfer of power to themselves. The famous film *Xala* by the Senegalese director Ousmane Sembéne revealed how new governments were started with briefcases of cash handed over by the remaining colonial civil servants. If the dictators who emerged had allocated even part of that money to fund modest old-age pensions for their citizens, instead of banking it in personal accounts in Switzerland, this would have released money into their own economies. Instead they bought weapons from Western arms traders. Of course, this needed collusion from the West. Some conformity to the rules would have been better than such blatant corruption.

I spent a month in China shortly after anti-government protests had been crushed in Tiananmen Square (1989). I met a 93-year-old Chinese bishop who had not long been released after being imprisoned at the Communist takeover in 1948. Everything in China was busy, busy! The many cyclists – all wearing uniform worker suits – clearly had enough spare cash to buy ice lollies at street corners. The first thing I saw when exiting Shanghai Terminus was an advert for Mastercard. Whereas in India the Communists, some of whom, in West Bengal, were landowners, had made a mishmash of the principles of Communism, the Chinese, it appeared, could make even Communism work – at least from the point of view of trade and commerce. There was rice growing everywhere, even to the very edge of the road. But accounts were beginning to emerge of the human cost of Mao's revolution in rural places, and Tiananmen Square had made it clear that conformity to Communism hadn't solved all of the country's problems.

In 1990 Nelson Mandela was released after 27 years incarcerated in South Africa. As a prison chaplain I watched his walk to freedom with a great deal of emotion. It defied belief that anyone could suffer so much for his beliefs and come out with his head held high.

★★★

The year before I left Barlinnie I organised a ceilidh in my old parish of Penilee for the silver jubilee of my ordination. My friend, Reverend John Miller, preached eloquently on what he saw as my faithfulness to the mission of the Gospel despite my having changed jobs every five years. He had spent all his time as parish minister in Castlemilk. Despite my frequent change of ministries I was gratified that my basic obedience to the Gospel was still recognised.

When I finally left my role as prison chaplain in 1992, the Roman Catholic weekly, *The Tablet*, published my reflections on my 10 years at Barlinnie. 'We have inherited', I wrote, 'a prison system that is part of the old Poor Laws: it is mostly used for those who turn to violence and theft to get their way.' Throughout the time I was a chaplain, the Scottish prison population was remarkably stable, sitting at an average of about 5,000. This has almost doubled since I left. There has been an upsurge in jailing drug users and sex offenders. Prisons have also become dumping grounds for those affected by mental ill-health. Sentences are getting longer: judges feel obliged to hand out what the public regards as exemplary punishment. Jails are the last resort for those who otherwise cannot live in society. As long as that is the case, there is little chance of rehabilitation for those committed to a life of crime.

10

Barras

By 1992 Archbishop Winning regarded many of the clergy, correctly but to their dismay, as an obstacle to his plans to renew the Church in Glasgow. He wanted it to be more outward-facing to the world, as the Second Vatican Council had sought. Because he was their superior, they had to appear to go along with him but for most of them their heart was not in it. There had been little ongoing professional development for them. The problem for the archbishop was: how do you change minds in an organisation where the culture is one of rule-by-diktat? Most organisations are hierarchical and have to manage change from time to time. Winning's solution was to switch the clergy around. After 10 years in the prison system I made myself available to him for a return to parish work, and he assigned me to Calton.

St Alphonsus was a church in the middle of the Barras weekend market, in the heart of the parish. It specialised in very fast Sunday services, offering the so-called 'microwave Mass'. Despite their promise of obedience there was particular resistance by the priests in St Alphonsus to being changed. They said they were doing well and would rather continue. They organised a petition. Winning was having none of it. One of them had been there 23 years and he stripped the place when he left. He took the musicians and a fair number of attenders to his new parish. This was fortunate. The place needed a new start. It needed to be redirected to local needs. I looked forward to the challenge of becoming parish priest there.

The area was not far from the Broomielaw area of Glasgow, where many of the Irish had landed during the famine and subsequent years. For those who described themselves as Mass-going Catholics it was as if Vatican II hadn't happened – apart from Mass being in English. The mindset of the congregation could be described as 'Broomielaw Theology'. They had improved socially without updating their faith. It was the job of the clergy, they thought, to run the Church and manage the buildings. What else did priests have to do? The people were content to turn up at Mass, where everything was done for them – the priests were expected to do the heavy work of faith and deliver it to them once a week in pre-digested form. As J.D. Salinger put it: 'The difference in spiritual sorties between St Francis [of Assisi] and the average, highstrung, Sunday leper-kisser is only a vertical one.'

For some the faith of their childhood had turned to ashes. It was part of my job to see if it could be rekindled. The oldest tradition in the Christian Church is Easter. At St Alphonsus we tried to implement a 90-day religious programme of renewal called from Ashes to Fire. It treated the 40 days of Lent as preparation for renewal of Baptismal promises at the Easter Vigil. It was followed by the 50 days before Pentecost as a period of enlightenment for a better understanding of faith. Religion requires a motivating force to bridge the gap between the good feelings that come from taking part in Sunday worship and the return to ordinary life on Monday mornings.

My ambition, if I ever had charge of a parish, had always been to make the Bible available to the parishioners. The first half of Sunday Mass is three readings from the Scriptures. The Bible Society were pleased to provide copies of the Bible so that the congregation could follow along. I announced that for the first year Mass would be extended to half an hour. Within the year one third of the congregation who had become habituated to the quicker service had left. A woman who came from Edinburgh to the Barras and enjoyed the famous 'Fast Mass' said she wouldn't be back. To be fair, some of the parishioners were ready to do more than simply turn up at Mass. A parish council was started. My cousin, Brother Norbert, had retired from a lifetime teaching maths in Africa and was keen to assist. He was able to lead some of the services. Sister Cathy, of the Sisters of Notre Dame, who had joined the prison chaplaincy, became part of our parish ministry. She was available to advise women who came for help.

The church building had been extremely well maintained. The Stations of the Cross, however, were disproportionately large. Notre Dame Convent in Dumbarton was closing and was disposing of a smaller, more artistic set. By coincidence a church in Northern Ireland which was being restored after having been blown up was looking for older ones. A swap was arranged – to be done in the middle of the night. It was several weeks before one of the local worthies noticed the change and complained, too late for anything to be done. Because of the demolition of the tenements opposite the church, the porch was open to the river and its winds. A baffle was put in and the word Peace in five different languages was inscribed on the new glass. The church's Pugin sanctuary was surrounded by twelve saints, of whom no fewer than five were women. But there was no St Alphonsus. Contact was made with the local artists' colony and Anne Devine created an icon of the saint from a wooden board. One of the stained glass artists, Lorraine Lamond, created a stunning rose window.

Reverend Ian Fraser of Calton parish had been a community minister in Greenock and was keen on ecumenical cooperation. We started a dawn service on Easter Sunday morning in Glasgow Green down by the riverside. One year, at 6 a.m., we were asked by park rangers if we had permission to gather. Fortunately, there was a right of assembly that was long established in the Green. George Parsonage of the river's Humane Society provided a cross he had made from river debris. One year on Ash Wednesday an African priest studying locally offered to help. I was accused of bringing in a 'Paki'. Asian traders were just beginning to make inroads into the Barras market.

In 1996 it was the 150th anniversary of the opening of the parish. Remarkably, it coincided with the 300th anniversary of the birth of the parish patron, St Alphonsus Liguori, in Naples. Fifty of us travelled together to visit his birthplace and had a wonderful fortnight staying in nearby Salerno. There was a papal audience in Rome with a mention of pilgrims from 'Sant' Alfonso'. We visited Monte Cassino and were welcomed in one of the nearby villages by relatives of those who had emigrated to Scotland from there.

In Glasgow we had a Jubilee Mass at which it was said that the singing was up to Church of Scotland standard. That was praise indeed. There was so much lay participation that at one point the archbishop said: 'If I could get a word in edgeways.' The city granted a civic reception for 500. Tickets were given out on a first-come-first-served basis. Many of the parishioners were old

Labour stalwarts but one told me it was the first time she had been given anything by the City Fathers. A booklet for the occasion was written by the City Solicitor, whose grandparents were from Calton. Finally, since we had been using the Barrowland Ballroom on occasion through the good offices of a descendant of Maggie McIver (the founder of the Barras market and the Ballroom) and manager Tom Joyes, we had a great jubilee dance there. There was a standing invitation to gigs and, amongst other events, I saw the final concert of Deacon Blue in 1994, when the lead singer, Ricky Ross, gave the appearance of ascending up to heaven.

However, parish work had never really been my idea of being a priest. It had come into the Catholic Church in response to the Reformation, when local congregations had become the basic building block of Christian presence. This has its own importance. But much of it could be done without a priest or minister. We had to think of the needs of the wider Church in the world in terms of witness to justice and peace. In response to this, I took a group from the parish on retreat to Fort Augustus Abbey. The aim was to see how much they could take responsibility for without depending on what the priest could do for them.

At the beginning of the Christian Church it was Roman law that accepted Hebrew religion and fused it with Greek civilisation. This offered the basis of human respect within the framework of empire. On the one hand the Greco-Roman view was that the law could only operate through the intelligentsia. On the other hand, the civil laws that derive in their origin from Church law support equality and reciprocity; the central insight of Christianity is egalitarian. Rights to the Kingdom of God are joined to duties towards others. For sure, within the Church a negative kind of Phariseeism has often enough raised its head. Although the Pope has the title 'Servant of the servants of God', rules and regulations created a hierarchy where individuals felt squashed. The education that had become widely available should have allowed priests to serve rather than having to lead.

***

After Christmas in 1991, I could hardly get myself out of bed. When I went to the osteopath he asked if I thought I had the weight of the world on my shoulders! It was clearly time to leave St Alphonsus. Although I had tried to share the burden, I had also taken on too much myself. It was hard work trying to persuade and teach others to take responsibility. Sometimes, alas, it was quicker and easier to do it oneself. I felt myself conforming to the expectations others had of what a parish priest should do.

My efforts in St Alphonsus could hardly be described as successful. Appearances were freshened up but people knew if a less ambitious priest came things would settle down again more or less as they had been. We got nowhere faster than the rest! In the Catholic Church the changes following the Second Vatican Council proved to be traumatic. They were long overdue, so it is hard to see how they could have been more gradual. However, there is no doubt the changes had a deleterious effect on the Church, not only in numbers but also in morale. Of course, this was true of other churches too. Only the independent, more charismatic type of congregations appeared to be holding their own. They did not put a premium on obedience or conformity.

A visit to an enclosed nun produced a nugget of wisdom. I must have been complaining about one thing or another. She said to me: 'Willy, changing yourself is the work of a lifetime; changing other people is the road to the madhouse.' There had been the opportunity to change the Church. Did churchgoers want it changed? Or was it me that wanted to change others without necessarily changing myself? The Apostolic Visitation to Ireland ordered by Pope Benedict XVI in 2010 noted 'a certain tendency … fairly widespread . . . among priests, religious and laity to hold theological opinions at variance with the Magisterium'. There was outward conformity but a lack of compliance inwardly. Prospero Lambertini, who had been a poet before becoming Pope Benedict XIV, when asked how the Church worked had said: 'The Pope decides, the Cardinals debate, the people do what they want.'

One of the parishioners who had been born the same week as me died suddenly. This prompted an interest in 'grey ministry', spirituality for older people. Many more older people were now surviving. Their childhood faith was no longer sufficient. When I visited older people in their homes it was clear that some didn't believe much any longer. A sobering experience had been visiting the home of a parishioner who had served in the navy during the war. He had his picture in uniform on the wall. On it he had added: 'All for nowt'. There was an emphasis on the young – how different they were from their elders. The truth was that the old were also changing. Even from them conformity could no longer be taken for granted.

11

Babies

When in the spirit of obedience I went to the archbishop in 1997 to say that I wanted to give up parish ministry I had no idea what he would say. I thought he might play the old card of bad example, that it was ridiculous to give up after only five years. It wasn't exactly a good example to others who might be struggling with parish work. To my surprise he immediately asked if I would consider hospital ministry. The chaplain to the Yorkhill hospitals had left, citing pressure from the job. No other priest was willing to take on the job of the Queen Mother's Maternity and the Royal Hospital for Sick Children. 'Sick calls' (visits to the sick) were being passed on to the local parish. Once when no priest was available the parents had phoned Winning himself. Prominent members of the hospital staff were unhappy about the lack of a Catholic chaplain.

Dealing with mothers and babies was the last thing that I had expected to have to do. I couldn't imagine asking mothers in labour how they were getting on! My first visit to the hospital resulted in a friend handing over his newborn baby while he dashed to get a nurse for his wife. Hospital chaplaincy, however, would give me scope to continue with my other interests. I drew the line when the archbishop said he would find a presbytery for me to live in. I had enough priest friends who could offer me accommodation somewhere that suited me better. One of them, Sabatino Tedeschi, offered to share his presbytery in St Charles's, Kelvinside with me. He also gave me a bike he had never used. There was a cycle path from Kelvinside all the way into Yorkhill.

Yorkhill was still operating the system on which the NHS was founded. The business management model by which doctors had to account to others had yet to be introduced. Some of the staff had been there all their lives. There were children who had lived in the hospital for years. Everyone knew everyone else. It was a congenial atmosphere to enter into. The main drawback was that the priest was seen as the last resort. When all else failed it was time for the 'last sacraments'. One day grandparents, seeing me at the entrance, were relieved to find out I had not been sent for to see their grandchild. It was difficult for me to reduce myself to the low expectations of a 'national disease service'. However, when the business management model was introduced, the continuity of care was affected. The old-fashioned way of looking after children throughout their lives gave way to separate specialisms. It was said the new doctors knew a great deal about very little.

Basically, what the hospital wanted was an on-call priest. The hospital chapel was revealing. It was not clear whether it was for services for the living or a memorial to the children who had died. Some hospitals had chapels with symbols from all religions. Others had no decoration at all in an attempt to remain 'neutral'. The greatest users of the Yorkhill chapel were individual Muslim members of staff saying their prayers. At Christmas Santa was the star. The switchboard operators became my best friends because they were the ones most able to decide if and when I was really needed.

Due partly to the legacy of Ian Donald, Professor of Midwifery at Glasgow University and pioneer of prenatal ultrasound scanning at the Queen Mother's Maternity Hospital, abortion didn't happen. Rather the opposite. There were desperate attempts to keep alive premature babies, some of whom were born just about the 24-week limit for legal abortion. 'Therapeutic' abortions were carried out in the Western Infirmary across the road. Occasionally we had cases where the baby was not going to survive infancy and the pregnancy was terminated. The chaplain was sometimes asked to give a blessing in such cases. My habit was 'don't ask, don't tell'. I felt it would serve no purpose to pry into the circumstances of the abortion. It was extremely painful for the parents to think of what was for them a profound loss. They were, of course, aware of what the Church said but, when they approached me, wanted and expected the consolation of prayer. Mothers in these cases needed all the help they could get. Neither society nor the Church had paid much attention to the question of abortion of babies that weren't going to survive birth. At that time the hospital was still talking about foetal 'disposal'. Older women told me they had never seen their stillborn baby. The Catholic Church, for all its stand against legal abortion, had no services for miscarriages.

Funerals for babies were common. I usually took the opportunity to mention how my mother had lost her first child and had never been able to speak about it to me, even after I was ordained. Many older women appreciated how this had been the case until recently. Women in NHS management helped with the change towards a better appreciation of the experience of bereaved mothers. They knew it was important that the event be recognised. One staff member was looking at the records one day beside the chaplaincy. I asked her if it was for a patient. No, she said, it was for herself. I asked when she lost the child. 'Seventeen years ago and yesterday,' she said. If parents were religious I read the story of King David, who fasted when his baby was sick and ate again when it died. According to the biblical account, he explained to his astonished friends: 'He will not come back to me but I will go to him.'

I liked the work and decided I should apply for an official chaplain's post advertised for a hospital nearby. I was surprised to discover that my application was not accepted. These posts were advertised for clergy of any denomination but interviews were managed by the Church of Scotland. Only 'Protestants' were appointed. The Catholic bishops went along with this because they were not keen to have priests earning a salary or committed full-time to a hospital. Catholic priests received only a modest honorarium for hospital chaplaincy. The status quo suited everybody. I was offered an interview for a psychiatric hospital where I was asked my views on abortion, which was probably the least likely eventuality there. I was advised by the interviewers to stay in Yorkhill, where the staff appreciated my free service.

I was still living in St Charles's when it celebrated its centenary, and the perspective made it possible for me to see what had gone wrong in the Church. The building was a beached whale. There had been a small church, albeit with a large school run by the Sisters of Notre Dame, which had served the purposes of Catholics in leafy Kelvinside. A decision was made to demolish the small church and build an enormous Coia one – on 20-foot piles and with a tower that looked like a minaret. Access to the church was difficult. The archdiocese had not yet reached the stage when a car park, or at least a bus stop, was considered necessary. At the centenary I was asked to try and clear the traffic jam in the one-way road system. In the line of cars was the famous lawyer Donald Finlay, whose house was nearby. He said he would park his car on top of another one.

Eventually the Queen Mother's Maternity was amalgamated with the Royal Infirmary, and the Children's Hospital transferred to the new super hospital at the Southern General site. I was asked to preach at the closing of Yorkhill, which was a great privilege. It was an opportunity to recognise the selfless work of staff for over a century. Before the National Health Service was introduced the doctors had given their services for children free.

Some chaplains felt there was not enough recognition for the work they themselves did. Some wanted to be treated as fellow professionals. It might have been more apt to remember the old Greek sage Diogenes. He ate only lentil soup. He was told if he was more subservient to the king he could eat all he wanted. He said that by living off soup he didn't have to be subservient to anyone. Chaplains to any institution need to be free from the expectations of conformity which could be put upon them.

12

Basilica

A new parish priest was appointed to St Charles's in 2001. Without so much as mentioning it, he brought an untrained dog into the house. Obedience to canine whims proved too much for me. It was time to look for a flat nearer the hospital. Out of the blue, the priest at St Simon's, the little church beside Yorkhill, as perjink a fellow as you would meet in a day's walk, was rushed to hospital with a stroke. He was the model of obedience but appeared to be unsympathetic to Vatican II. His model of a priest was St John Vianney who, after the 1789 French Revolution, was the Curé d'Ars (the parish priest of Ars, a remote village), where he tried to get the Church to return to more religious ways. When I heard what had happened I went to St Simon's to see if I could help. That night the empty house was broken into. The housekeeper asked me to take the keys. I phoned the archdiocese, offering to stay. It suited them to have temporary cover until the parish priest, Father Chalmers, returned. It turned out to be for the remaining 12 years of my ministry, since he never became fit enough to resume duties.

The previous parish priest, Father Paddy Tierney, who had been brought up locally, had saved the old church from being demolished when the surrounding area was cleared of its tenements. Paddy was a maverick who disagreed with the centralising tendency of the diocese. Having refurbished St Simon's he attracted large crowds by his anti-establishment approach. He was a Church historian and had been invited in 1978 to give the anniversary lecture in front of the bishops on the occasion of the centenary of the restoration of the Scottish Catholic Hierarchy. He greatly irritated them by opining that three bishops were plenty for Scotland rather than the present eight. He died prematurely since, as the saying goes, he did not look after himself. He also neglected to maintain the church fabric. With some difficulty I persuaded Cardinal Winning to visit St Simon's in its run-down state. He looked weary, and confided how hard he found it to make priests change their habits. He died of a sudden heart attack a few months later.

St Simon's had become known in Glasgow as the Polish Church. Some people thought the Poles had built it, although it dated from 1858. During World War Two members of the Polish Army who had escaped from Nazi occupation reached Britain. One of the camps training them to join the D-Day invasion was at Yorkhill, so they attended the nearest Catholic church, which was the Partickbridge Street building (then known as old St Peter's but to become St Simon's). When the war finished they were told to find a place of their own. They worshipped at the disused St Bride's in Cheapside Street until Paddy Tierney, seeking to build up his congregation, invited them back to St Simon's.

The archbishop (Mario Conti) said he wanted to run by me the idea of handing St Simon's over to the Polish community. Unlike in England, the Poles in Scotland did not have their own churches. Their needs were met by three chaplains who travelled around; the chaplain responsible for Glasgow was not keen to take over a church. He had been in post since 1974 and had seen his congregation steadily shrinking since the war, between death of the veterans and the loss of cultural contact by younger people.

Then in 2004 Polish immigrants from the EU began to arrive in the UK. The new arrivals completely swamped St Simon's. The Polish chaplain was not bothered that they had to stand outside in the rain – he said that was what they did in Poland. The obvious answer would have been to move them down the road to the larger St Patrick's, in Anderston. Most of the population there had been cleared out by the building of the motorway. Unfortunately, a Polish woman had been murdered there by the serial killer Peter Tobin, who had been permitted to frequent the premises. She had been buried under the floorboards of the church. In the circumstances it was not going to be a church the Poles could use. The parish priest of St Patrick's had obviously not been supervised and received little official support in his difficulties. He was severely censured during the court case, at which the diocese was conspicuous by its absence.

The Poles arriving from the EU needed a place where they

could meet each other and worship together. In their homeland the Catholic Church provided such venues. The Polish Club in Glasgow proved too small. Strangely, I thought, I was asked why they didn't worship in English. This from people who were still proud of their Irish origins only a generation or two earlier. I started to attend Polish language classes. The Polish chaplain enabled me to visit Poland to see the birthplace of John Paul II. I took the opportunity to visit Auschwitz. It was a sobering experience. The Holocaust, being so recent, changes one's perspective on good and evil. It gives a glimpse of how ordinary people can do evil. As Clive James noted (in *Cultural Amnesia*), half the Polish intelligentsia had been murdered by one set of madmen (the Nazis) and half by another set (the Soviets). Though some survived in body, their hearts were broken. Their children and grandchildren remembered their suffering.

When the Polish Pope died in 2005 I got a phone call at 11 p.m., a couple of hours later, to ask why 'the Polish church' was not open. Next morning at 7 a.m. I was asked what time special services would be. By 8 a.m. the media was camped outside the door. Coverage of the funeral of John Paul II was total in St Simon's – partly celebrity worship of a global figure and partly recognition of an icon of authority.

The archdiocese had done nothing for the new Poles. Other dioceses had taken on Polish priests. St Simon's, the smallest church in the city, ended up with the biggest attendance in the diocese. Meanwhile the congregation at nearby St Peter's had halved in a decade; families were leaving the congested West End. Unexpectedly, its parish priest retired. I wrote to the archbishop to say that the new parish priest should be willing to take some responsibility for the expanding Polish congregation. 'You are the very man for that,' he replied. I was attending an Emmaus conference in war-torn Sarajevo when I was appointed parish priest also of St Peter's. I thus found myself in charge of two parishes. When I first outlined my plans for the parishes to the happy-go-lucky assistant at St Peter's he nearly had a nervous breakdown.

My ambition was to unite the two churches. They were on either side of a main road. Although St Peter's was on a busy street, it was closed during the day. After much argument I was able to get it open again. In the movies Catholic churches are always open for people to light a candle. It is worth asking who started closing them. Presumably it was to prevent stealing, although the only precious object is the reserved sacrament – something no one can make financial gain from. Priests in more difficult areas were reopening their churches. One said he got more money from people lighting candles than he lost in petty vandalism.

In a way bringing the two churches together would have completed a circle. Between 1903 and 1945 Partick had two churches but only one parish. The big one, St Peter's, used the smaller one as an annexe. I did take both parish councils away for a day together but the different needs of the two churches were too great. St Simon's was small enough almost to run itself. When I took over St Peter's I was surprised to discover that not only did it not have any money in the bank, it was in debt because of the decoration for the centenary of the building in 2003. That money would have been better spent on a survey of the fabric, which had the usual problems of a 100-year-old building. The heating system only worked by one of the Marist Brothers being on hand to reignite it. A generous donation allowed us to instal new boilers in St Peter's.

Some in St Peter's were not keen to accommodate the Poles. Others thought it great to see the church busier again, especially with younger people. I wrote up the history of both churches, prompted by a lecture given by Ranald MacInnes of Historic Scotland as part of the West End Festival on the history of the two Catholic churches in Partick. When the parish held its 150th anniversary, some did not believe it was older than the church building, which was only 100 years old. The parish chairwoman, who was in this camp, declined to have anything to do with the parish anniversary, and the choir absented itself from the celebratory Mass, since the anniversary was on a bank holiday. The archbishop came first to St Simon's (the old St Peter's) and then was piped across the road for a second Mass in (the new) St Peter's. A week later we had a civic reception for both parishes in the City Chambers. Everyone in St Simon's had used St Peter's but some in St Peter's boasted of never having been in St Simon's.

After many years of other kinds of ministry I found myself once more having to visit the local Catholic schools. They were under tremendous pressure to fulfil the new curriculum requirements of the Scottish Government. The teaching of religion was inevitably squeezed. Some of the teachers were less interested in doctrinal formation. They saw activities sponsored by organisations like the Scottish Catholic International Aid Fund (SCIAF) during Lent as being more practical. It could lead to a rather sentimental morality. The pupils, finding Mass not well done, ceased to attend church and saved their money for gigs. The risk was well known of 'sacramentalising the unevangelised'; some continued to practise their faith while others were detached and a few became opposed to it.

After a couple of years, without saying anything to me, Archbishop Conti arranged for another priest to take over St Peter's if I was willing to stand aside. I had made it clear I was willing to resign from both parishes, but he only wanted me to leave St Peter's. The new man showed himself to be uninterested in St Simon's. So we were back to where we had started with the two churches separate again. The archbishop expressed his gratitude to me, but I had been used to get him out of a difficult position when he was struggling to find a parish priest for St Peter's. I had once expressed to him the need for self-appraisal among the clergy. I had shown him the appraisal form I had to complete as chair of a voluntary organisation but he missed the point and simply thought I was providing information about my own activities. There was no sense in the Church of a need for the clergy to audit themselves, that is, to say what they should be doing and have some measure as to whether they had done it or not.

Eventually a new archbishop did appear to succeed Mario Conti. He also had an Italian name – Philip Tartaglia. One of his first acts was to send out a circular asking that, if priests wanted a change or to retire, they should contact his secretary. I made an appointment to see him. Although I was 18 months short of the official retirement age of 75 he made no objection to my leaving early. He only said he wasn't keen on having what he described as a 'people's republic' in a parish! The timing of my retirement suited us both. I had been 12 years in St Simon's, the longest I had lived anywhere. He needed to know, reasonably enough, how many priests he could rely on to obey him as he began his episcopate.

A visiting missionary said the good atmosphere in St Simon's had not been easily achieved. At a Scots College Annual Dinner I was asked – possibly tongue-in-cheek – to propose the toast to the Hierarchy. I told the audience I had never spoken to a bishop until after I was ordained. They thought that explained a lot! I also said a good bishop wouldn't make me a good priest nor a bad bishop make me a bad priest. One of the ancient writers had said the biggest danger to monks were women and bishops! My faith was not in prelates.

In the *Glasgow Herald* I found myself nominated as a radical priest and one of the Ten Top Tims in Scotland. I always thought 'radical priest' was a contradiction in terms. A priest as such is part of the system. Yet he does have the chance to get to the root of things. I was described as a non-conformist in a hierarchical society. It was a fair description but it meant I had to accept the consequences, one of which was that I could easily be replaced.

13

Blessing?

What if my mother had got her way? After the war she had wanted to return to Bristol. Photographs show that we had had a well-appointed terraced house. We would have received a religious upbringing from her. England, however, might have been less hospitable than Scotland to an exclusively Catholic education. Would I have been invited by a priest to study for the priesthood? My cousins in England had an equally devout Catholic mother and went to Catholic schools but have not retained their religious denomination. There the Christian tradition has become 'untethered'.

The first Christians were accused of atheism. They did not believe in the Roman gods. Justin Martyr was one of the first educated people to join them. He was a philosopher. He was asked by the emperor to give some account of what this new group were up to. Justin said they were 'people of the book', as were their Jewish ancestors before them (and the Muslims after them). When they gathered together it was to listen to the writings of those who had witnessed the Resurrection of their Lord, Jesus Christ. They pledged obedience to him and him alone. They followed The Way mapped out by him. They had no desire to disobey the laws of the empire but were prepared to suffer for their beliefs. Justin was beheaded for his pains.

Christians, including Roman Catholics, when they gather on a Sunday, listen first of all to The Word, the Bible. Faith is obedience to The Other, the Creator, the Father who does not speak. If obedience is not to be reduced to conformity it has to be a listening-out for something different – the sound of The Other which comes to us in our conscience. It is an act of faith. It shows a challenging way, full of obstacles, which eventually strips us down towards our real self. Without the habit of such reflection we run the risk of being subject to hallucination – making things up by ourselves.

St Paul said: 'For the good that I would I do not: but the evil which I would not, that I do' (Romans 7:19). One priest, when told that someone didn't attend church because it was full of hypocrites, said it wasn't – there was room for more! Most people are not consciously hypocritical but they find themselves faced with choices. The tenor of the age is that we are free to do whatever we want. But this is not true. Whether one is a shop assistant or a sheriff, choices have to be made. Some may be routine but others could put one's job at risk. This could become more important than making the right decision. My party piece is 'Holy Willie's Prayer' by Robert Burns. Willie was a zealous hypocrite. The poem is a sobering reflection on how we can conform to social expectations. Not many have the singlemindedness of the Scottish poet Hugh MacDiarmid. He was welcomed to his new home in Biggar by being invited to a Burns Supper. He ruined everything by declining to stand for the Loyal Toast.

The proliferation of Christian denominations after the Reformation made it harder for people to be blindly obedient to the Church. State law started to take precedence. But the State was not truly secular; it took on the role of the sacred. This was interpreted as *roi, loi, foi* (king, law, faith). The State did not so much exist as was believed in. Faith in the State required conformity to its diktats. It was the State that was charged with the maintenance of a secular faith. The collapse of the Church in Scotland – of all denominations – created a vacuum which the Holyrood Parliament has sought to fill since 1999. The Church was thought to be prescriptive, but governments became even more directive. Political correctness became the name of the game. In liberal societies, to be religious was to be deemed conservative. But religion, in fact, offered some independence from the mainstream. Churches are voluntary organisations. Essentially, they depend on personal contact.

In 1938 E.M. Foster wrote that 'the more highly public life is organised the lower does its public morality sink'. Fascism demonstrated this. German National Christians were, for the most part, Protestant agnostics or social atheists. They experienced no real demand to obey the precepts associated with their religion. Totalitarianism demanded conformity with the State.

Obedience is thought to be doing what you are told, either by another person or according to the dictates of one's own conscience. The etymology of the word obedience is the Latin *ob-audire*, which means to listen. Not many get the chance to listen to their own conscience. They have to do what they are told by others. Life becomes a series of compromises between what we would like to do and what we have to do. 'A man's got to do what a man's got to do' is the saying. All sorts of influences wield their power over us.

What marks out the Roman Catholic priest is his obedience to a singular human authority, not the Pope but the bishop. Most people are obedient most of the time to human authority, whether they would like to admit it or not. The question is whether it is really obedience or just conformity? Do most people have to go along with what is happening, whether it is slavery, fascism or consumerism? My first experience living among professional people in Glasgow's West End was quite a shock. They had well-paid jobs. It didn't pay for them to question what they were doing. They didn't read widely and so mostly they didn't question themselves. In private some might be cynical, but that wasn't enough.

According to Pope Francis, Christian living is not about obeying rules. It is about changing oneself, not others. We need a cut-down Church. This does not mean a Church of the most devout, but a gathering of those who experience Christian faith as a risk and are prepared to put it into practice. Most keep their heads down. But some do take risks. The Church should support the risk-takers. Inasmuch as we all have to conform to the expectations of others, then obeying the demands of the Gospel should be something that can be understood and judged as such. The defining mark for anyone is not an outward conformity but a belief in a Higher Power to which one is ultimately answerable. For most people this is mediated through family and work. We have not to look back on a life of obeying the law but to look forward to revelation promised by Jesus.

Do priests just conform to what is expected of them? The word episcopal comes from *epi-skopos*, which is the Greek equivalent of the Latin *super-visor*. Clergy are probably as careless in the eyes of their supervisor as the average worker. But systems are only successful if the staff are also able to show initiative and creativity. It is not the image that the Church gives most of the time. My experience of fellow clergy is that they were not strong on initiative. 'It has always been done this way' was the refrain. It is interesting to reflect that at the Reformation, the Catholic Church in Scotland collapsed not because of the immorality of the clergy but because priests found it easier to obey the new authorities. I believed myself to be part of an international movement where the members were able to witness to the Gospel, irrespective of what bishops might or might not do.

Of course, as in society so in the Church, some are promoted beyond their level of competence. There is deep ecclesiastical conservatism. Bishops see themselves as managers of Church property but they are not very good managers. Cardinal Marx, Archbishop of Munich – probably the richest diocese in the Catholic Church – speaking in 2016 about the episcopal office, didn't think they were even good defenders of the deposit of faith. Some want to take the credit for things they haven't done and avoid blame when the responsibility is theirs. The truth is they have had no training for the job of being bishop. They don't feel any responsibility for the present state of the Church. They are picked for their record of conformity, understood as obedience. They then find some ideal of professional behaviour. However, the way the Church actually works is that someone has to be in charge, and for Catholics that person is the bishop. There are few opportunities for those who can't accept that mundane reality.

In *The Ministry of the Printed Word* (2016), Broadley and Phillips looked at the effect of obedience on some well-known priests in England. Several of them were converts to Catholicism and therefore hadn't had a strict seminary experience. They were well off and relatively independent. Among them the Jesuit George Tyrrell was excommunicated in 1900 as a 'Modernist' and the Benedictine David Knowles, history professor at Cambridge, suffered a similar fate in 1955. The cradle Catholic and secular priest Peter Hughes, who was ordained in 1925, wrote a magisterial history of the English Catholic Church but got no support from his own bishop and had to be rescued from parish work by Notre Dame University in America. In their days obedience was *the* criterion.

It was sometimes said I did not get on with bishops. Obedience is more than a willingness to be moved to another job to suit a superior. There are times when the bishops don't get it. At those times the Church finds itself becalmed. Fortunately there is a certain anarchy in the Catholic Church. The Spirit is given to all the baptised. This fits in with Chaos Theory. Perhaps there was more tolerance of chaos in earlier times. Religious orders became influential because they were international and were able to go beyond the limited outlook of local bishops.

When I was paid for what I was doing – whether as a psychologist or a chaplain – there was talk among colleagues at work of changing things, but not at the risk of losing their job. In each field there were a few who tried to stretch the terms of their employment and who went out of their way to make a difference. The system was usually strong enough to absorb even those who would like to think they were dissidents. A neat example is airport security. No matter what we are asked to do, we go along with it without protest as if we were sheep. And that is just to get on a plane.

I was accused of being 'contrary', going against the grain, that I wasn't a team player, that I was an individualist. Reflecting on it all, the best that was said of me was that I was 'my own man' and that I was not afraid to speak up. Bangladesh, in particular, was a catalyst. First of all I was silenced for the first year while I learned the language. Secondly, I had to look out for myself. I don't think there was much physical fear but I had to find a new niche. After I returned from Bangladesh friends hesitated to question me. The experience there seemed quite remote from their daily experience. I don't think I rammed it down other people's throats but they might have thought I would.

A Canadian oblate of Mary Immaculate, who had been a missionary to the Inuit was appointed to a wealthy parish in Montreal. He wrote a poem about his new assignment:

> In a nice church / with nice candles / and nice flowers /
>   on a nice altar
> A nice priest / in nice vestments / read a nice gospel / and
>   said a nice Mass
> For nice people / nicely dressed / sitting in nice pews

Who said nice prayers / to a nice Jesus / who had a nice
   birth / a nice life / a nice death / a nice resurrection
And now sits nicely / in a nice heaven / with a nice Father
It was so nice.

I wasn't subject to demands to conform. Indeed I had acquired,
apparently, a reputation by which I was expected to question the
status quo and 'stir things up'. Fortunately I had enough friends
to prevent me from turning into a complete crank. At the end of
the day I have to ask myself whether I did enough. Absolutely
not, would have to be the answer. There is a wonderful story of
an old abbot talking to a young monk who was telling him that
he had obeyed all the monastic rules. Now, what else should he
do, he asked? The old abbot asked: 'Have you ever thought of
setting yourself on fire?' There were occasions when I wondered
if setting myself on fire might help. I lacked the moral courage of
the Buddhist monks protesting in Vietnam. A Catholic Worker
member had set himself on fire in New York. I was conditioned
by what I thought were the necessities of a couple of square meals
each day and a bed at night.

In my review (in *Open House*, 2003) of Cardinal Winning's
biography, *This Turbulent Priest* by Stephen McGinty, I noted how
little time he had ever found to relate with his priests who were
also his colleagues. Many bishops don't put relationships with their
priests as a priority. Priests in their turn strive mostly to 'lie low'.
I once found myself left alone to do some research on justice and
peace in the archives of the archdiocesan office. I was tempted
to look up my own file. I didn't do so, because I suspected there
would be very little in it. It would probably just be a list of appointments. In the archdiocese of Glasgow when a priest dies a purely
functional notice of funeral arrangements is published. There is no
mention of whether he served long or short stints, did well or not
so well.

When I retired I was sometimes asked if I continued to say
Mass each day. Daily Mass is a devotion which can be traced back
to pre-Reformation times but it's not widely known that priests, if
they are in charge of a parish, have a requirement to say Mass for
the parishioners only on a Sunday. They don't have any other obli-
gation. So if a priest is not in charge of a parish he is free to take

his place in the pews like anyone else. The absence of daily Mass gives a false sense that there is a shortage of priests. In missionary countries, where the missionary has great distances to cover, people usually don't have the chance to attend Mass even on a Sunday.

***

The great example of conformity for most of us is the once every five years or so right to vote. We usually do this according to the cultural norms of which we are a part. So it is that the majority of those who vote are older. I have come to the conclusion that if young people are deemed unable to vote until they are 16 or 18 it should be considered inappropriate at a certain age for older people to vote, because they are unlikely to live to see the consequences of their choice. I would propose that nobody is given the vote after 75, the age at which they are entitled to a free TV licence. Children have to accept the consequences of how their parents vote. There comes a time when the parents should be willing to live according to the decisions not only of their children but also of their grandchildren. Why should older people vote to leave the UK or Europe when it is their children and grandchildren who will have to live with the consequences?

One of the great films of recent times, *Of Gods and Men* (2010), is about the dilemma of the French Trappists monks in Algeria during the civil war after the army had advised them to leave. They voted to stay and paid with their lives. It was an example of obedience to a higher cause even to the point of death. Some kind of suffering is the risk involved in obedience to the Gospel. Inasmuch as we all have to conform to the expectations of others, then conforming to the life of Jesus is a choice. We have the opportunity to edge the door a little more open for the sake of others – or to close it a little to make ourselves more comfortable. Pushing the door open is a risky business. Being obedient to one's conscience will always suggest one should have a belief that it is worthwhile putting one's shoulder to the door.

When older people get the chance to express regret about what they have done or not done with their lives they will perhaps say that they gave too much energy to paid work. In other words, for the time they had to do what they were told. So retirement can be a privileged time if it is not taken up entirely by having to care for others. It might be passed going on holiday, living for grandchildren or keeping an eye on the bank balance. But it can also be a call back to our true selves. In what or whom did we put our faith, we might ask? The Word we might have heard in our hearts does not tell us what to do, but is a listening to the deepest questions we have about ourselves and the world.

Part 2
Poverty

14

Origins

My birthday, 17 January, is the feast of St Anthony of Egypt (the saint who helps us find things is St Anthony of Padua). Anthony was a rich young man who about AD 250 gave up his inheritance to go and live an ascetic life in Sinai. He is one of the first of the 'Desert Fathers', the wise men of the east. The early Christians tended to be urban, i.e. living in cities, different from the *pagani* (pagans), meaning country dwellers. There was among some of the citizens at the time, however, a hankering after a more literal following of the Gospel. They followed Anthony and others out into remote places.

Anthony is regarded as the founder of monasticism, the pursuit by monks and nuns of obedience, poverty and celibacy. He is the first subject of a biography of a saint. It was written by one of his followers, Athanasius of Alexandria. Anthony lived for a while as a hermit. He practised the Greek axiom: 'know thyself'. Eventually so many joined him that he had to return to community life. He set up monasteries for those who wanted to embrace the Gospels more literally. 'To know oneself well one should be stripped of all that is not essential,' he said. Embracing poverty was for him a step towards this.

The Jewish Messiah had been expected to appear as a model of obedience to the Law and not as a model of poverty. Jesus of Nazareth came as an outsider, a highlander from the hills of Galilee. Traditionally, he was born in a stable. According to the Gospels he had nowhere to lay his head. The greatest story told about him, unusually recorded in all four Gospels, was of his providing food for those who had none at the feeding of the 5,000. He was looked down on by the establishment in Jerusalem. He died the death of a criminal on a cross. Whatever else might be said about him, he was definitely poor.

Throughout history most people have been poor but, perhaps for that reason, poverty itself has not been prized. In the Christian Church wealth has been a factor in its progress. The Vatican is notoriously rich. Yet the Catholic Church has always had its biggest following among the poor. A minority, following the monastic tradition dating back to St Anthony, has embraced voluntarily the poverty of Jesus. Poverty, one would think, ought to be a defining characteristic of Christian faith.

Photographs of children in Glasgow in the 1940s tell a story of poverty. They look different from today. The full range of clothing from the respectable to the ragged is visible. Open mouths reveal gaps in teeth. There were squints and the traces of rickets. There is not a hint of obesity. That was the reserve of the well-off, like the comic character Billy Bunter. In Scotland only now are researchers beginning to study what is called the 'Glasgow effect' of urban poverty. Glasgow became the Second City of the Empire from the tobacco trade and then the sugar trade, both powered by slavery overseas. Scottish and Irish peasants were removed from the land and turned into industrial workers. There followed the ruthless control of income, housing and education. It was a long struggle before these workers were able to command a living wage. The inheritance of Red Clydeside lived on in deprivation. If Glasgow, with respect to health, were removed from the national statistics, Scotland would appear as an average country instead of one with some of the worst averages in Europe.

In Penilee there weren't any rich or fat people, nor many who were poor and thin. Growing up we knew little if anything either of the stinking rich or the stinking poor. Both my grandfathers were classed as skilled workers. Before marriage my father lived in a terraced house. My mother was born in Cowlairs single-storey housing built for railway workers and known as 'the blocks'. As a Rolls-Royce toolmaker my father was at the top of his trade. I never lived in a house without a bathroom. There must have been leftovers from meals because a separate 'pig bin' lorry collected waste food. My father paid his union dues. My mother was a stalwart of the Tenants' Association. She ran a 'menodge' (from the French *ménage*, meaning thrift), which collected a shilling from other housewives and paid out the whole sum to each as they drew lots. A couple of pounds would have been significant at that time. Both my parents voted Labour. The motto of the Labour Party could be described as onward and upward for the working class. Everyone had to work. Everyone would get on.

During World War Two, peace was a more urgent need than economic prosperity. My very first memory is of being held by a soldier in a railway station as my mother tried to negotiate wartime travel between Bristol and Glasgow. There was a barrage balloon that protected the factories in Hillington Estate. There has often come into my mind the thought that something beside me could suddenly explode. I have wondered if this is part of the inheritance of having spent my first months in an air-raid shelter. In my mind still is a childhood chant: 'V for victory, dot dot dash, Hitler lost his wee moustache, when he fun [found] it, he lost his bunnet [cap], V for victory, dot dot dash.' We belonged to the winning side, no doubt about that. My brother was named Michael Victor, my mother sure she would see off Hitler. She had lost a child together with her first husband in the 1928–29 influenza epidemic, and called my sister Anne Morag after her (as was the custom of the time, my mother never spoke about this loss, but she kept a photo of Morag aged about five). I was called William after my grandfather. My mother added John because she didn't want me called Billy and John was how I was (am) known in the family.

I have often been asked if the name Slavin is Polish. It is from the Gaelic *sleive*, meaning mountain. My paternal grandfather commuted between the potteries in his native Belleek and Glasgow. My father got some of his schooling in Ireland and had the highest praise for the single teacher, Master McGovern. My mother claimed to be 'Scotch to the backbone'. My father was keen that she was at home for the children and didn't want her to go out to work. She solved that by eventually getting a night-shift job as cashier in the Hillington Estate canteen. Even as an engineer my father's income would have been as little as the company could get away with. Mother's wage made choices possible.

They were hungry for the success that would allow their children to progress. My parents didn't work to make a profit but no value was attached to poverty. Little or nothing was appreciated of destitution in other parts of the world. A set of encyclopedias was bought from a travelling salesman. This described the British Empire as progressive. The effects of the war against Fascism would ultimately benefit everybody. If, for me, poverty remained a virtue or ideal it might somehow be attributed to the saint on whose feast day I was born.

15

Housing Scheme

Penilee was a housing estate or 'scheme'. The houses were rented from Glasgow Corporation. Since the area was low-lying there were problems with dampness. Skilled workers were not well paid but they were not poor. Father enjoyed his 'half (of whisky) and a half pint' on a Friday night. Overtime work on Tuesdays and Thursdays allowed him to indulge himself more generously. The fact that everyone rented their house helped with a sense of solidarity among 'the tenants'. In contemporary social commentaries it is easy to spot those who went to posh schools: they confuse the working class with the poor.

For a 'war baby' there was rationing, which was a major feature of life in Britain during and after the Second World War. Until the early 1950s it affected everything from clothes to sweets. Observers since have argued that it provided a balanced diet. Someone, presumably 'high up', had worked out how much food people needed in order to sustain the war effort. This guaranteed that everyone had enough to eat. It might have been plain but there was sufficient variety to stimulate the palate. Children still had to be encouraged to clean their plate, being reminded of hungry children elsewhere. My mother was not particularly interested in cooking but was able to put homemade soup on the table followed by mince, cabbage, potatoes and the like. There was a garden and my father made efforts to grow vegetables in it. We were given pennies to put into the hand of the 'black baby' doll on the teacher's desk to help the starving overseas.

Rationing showed that the state could act if it felt the need, as it did in war. The *Beveridge Report* in 1942 (when life expectancy was 65 – which is why the pension age was fixed at that) spoke of 'giant evils' of want, disease, ignorance, squalor and idleness.

Beveridge proposed an extension to the insurance system that would provide protection against those evils. The economist R.H. Tawney, however, and his disciple Richard Titmuss, had more radical ideas about universal welfare, which persuaded people in the 1945 general election to ditch the war leader Churchill and vote for change. This allowed the Labour government to bring in ideas of welfare reform above and beyond the safety blanket provided by an insurance system.

As part of this the National Health Service was established in 1948. It was just in time for me. I had earache and breathed through my mouth. Neither my sister nor my brother was ever in hospital but I managed to get measles and was confined to Belvidere Fever Hospital, where patients could be seen from the verandas but visitors were not allowed to enter the wards. When I got out I was treated to a fire engine from a toy shop in Paisley. Otherwise my father made all our toys. He also cut our hair and repaired our shoes on an iron last he had made. We visited him in the Victoria Infirmary when he had pleurisy and were duly awed by its formality. I remember one of the last deaths from TB, a lovely girl in the next close.

There was perpetual noise from the Rolls-Royce engine test beds. At Hogmanay we stayed up to hear the bells of Paisley Abbey bringing in the New Year. We could hear the horns of the ships anchored on the River Clyde near Govan. These horns signalled to us one morning that King George VI had died. The centre of Penilee had been left as an open field which everyone could use and in which we would have a bonfire with a Guy (Fawkes), a sign of the beginning of winter. There were two good bus services, one to the city centre and the other to Govan, where many of the residents had come from. The Govan Fair was a highlight of the year. As we were close to the city boundary we could walk over the hill and get a fast bus to the city centre.

We were only allowed to shop in the PCMS Co-op (Paisley Cooperative Manufacturing Society). The dividend paid out to members twice a year bought our school uniforms and Sunday clothes. For many years the three of us were dressed identically. Our 'divi' number was 23626, which we always had to give when making purchases. Until the Cooperative opened in Penilee mother shopped in the Springburn Co-op and walked back over the unlit Penilee hill. In the winter dark she prayed the Rosary, she said. There were no pubs on Corporation housing, much to my father's chagrin. There were local polls to change this but my mother told him it was not worth his going to the polling station since she would be out behind him to keep the status quo.

The general feeling at the time was that you got what you needed. All our neighbours appeared to have the same standard of living. There was no sense that anyone had any more. Christmas wasn't celebrated in the way it is now in Scotland – in those days it was thought to be an English thing. Rolls-Royce, being an English firm, gave the child of every worker a substantial toy at Christmas. In summer we were expected to leave the house with 'ginger and pieces' (lemonade and sandwiches) and 'follow the leader' wherever he chose to go, sometimes as far as the River Cart, until we returned at tea-time. 'Wee Pete' Callaghan had a den in his garden that we were initiated into. My sister had her own room while I shared a bed with my brother. A great event was when 'the gas man' came and returned to the residents a fixed percentage of the pennies, which he counted out on the kitchen table.

There were hawkers who came round the doors and we were instructed to be polite to them whether we bought anything or not. These were the only non-white people we saw. We presumed they came from the countries of the British Empire we had read about. I once laughed at a neighbour who had a large family when she passed with a pram full of bread. I was told she kept her children clean, which was more important than food. The only serious poverty I saw as a child was when we were taken to Dublin and there were women and children begging in the streets. We had passed through Belfast and were shocked to see policemen with guns. There was a strict customs control at the Northern Ireland border and everyone seemed to accept the challenge of bringing contraband through without being caught. Irish linen was particularly valued.

My recollection is that while there was money for necessities, there was little extra. We had ice cream once a week from the van that toured the streets. Mother saved for an annual holiday. This was in Arran when we were small. After we had made First Communion we went elsewhere because at that time the land-owner didn't allow Catholic Mass. Before setting out from home

Mother would put a half crown under our statue of the Child of Prague to get us started again after the holidays. As we grew older, Mother liked to pick a different place each year for a summer holiday. Once we returned to Bristol. Another time we went to see my father's relatives in Belleek. He didn't know any who could put us up and Mother was much put out to have to pay for a hotel.

We knew nothing of the independence of India, the revolution in China, the foundation of Israel or even the descent of the Iron Curtain. Father got a piano before we could afford a radio. Once we did, in the evening we listened to 'Dick Barton Special Agent' before running out to various activities. Everyone tuned in to 'The MacFlannels', a stereotypical Scottish family show. Although the *Daily Express* was anti-socialist my father liked it for its feature by Beachcomber (J.B. Morton, brother of the travel writer H.V. Morton). On Sundays we were sent out to get the *Sunday Post*, the *Sunday Mail* and the *Reynolds News* (a Cooperative paper) together with 'ten Players or Capstan' cigarettes for my father. He had a fund of stories with a moral to them, like the one about the man returning to work after the Depression. The boss told him his tools were 'gey rusty'. 'You ought to see the bloody frying pan,' replied the man.

The housing estate also formed the Catholic parish. In Glasgow, Catholics were often allocated spare ground at the edge of a scheme on which to build a chapel. The result was that Our Lady and St George's backed onto private housing which was kept in Lourdes, the mother parish. Some children from the Nazareth House Orphanage in Cardonald came to school in Penilee. They were well, though distinctively, dressed. There was therefore a reverse kind of exclusiveness among the working class in the area, but this sense of community spirit was class- rather than faith-based.

There was one unusual intervention by the Church in local affairs. Rolls-Royce introduced a bonus scheme. The workers managed it so that everyone got extra money. One individual, however, 'Bonus Joe', went all out to make as much as he could. The union withdrew his card and wanted him sacked since they ran a closed shop – everyone was supposed to work at the same pace, so no one should work harder for bonuses. The company refused and a strike was called. It went on for some weeks and threatened to affect Christmas. Some of the shop stewards were Communists looking for a trial of strength against the bosses. Suddenly the Archbishop of Glasgow produced an anti-Communist pastoral letter saying it was necessary to get back to work to provide money for Christmas. The strike ended. There had been no such intervention by the Church before, nor was there another afterwards.

Doris Lessing, who arrived in Britain from South Africa in 1949, captured the spirit of the times in an interview in 2008 when she remembered: 'Nobody had any money, that's the point, nobody was rich.' Both wealth and poverty were to all intents and purposes invisible in the monoculture of the housing estate.

16

Boarding School

Blairs College was founded in 1829. It was the national junior seminary, where boys who aspired to be local priests had their secondary education. The best word to describe its condition would be frugal. But that wasn't what we thought at the time, since everyone was more or less the same. There was no uniform. The intention was to improve the mostly working-class boys who had thought of becoming priests. Most did well out of their education there, some going on later to distinguished pursuits. My two closest friends became leader of a local authority and a deputy head teacher respectively. A third emigrated to America and became the proud parent of two New York cops. Just as certain boarding schools that were meant to give the wealthier a better education and endow them with a sense of *noblesse oblige* towards the 'lower classes', Blairs College instilled in us Blairentians, as we called ourselves, the idea that we were to set an example to Catholics who had not enjoyed such an education.

The school year began with a three-day silent retreat. On our first arrival, no sooner had the bell struck for it to begin than the boy next to me whispered: 'Biggles breaks the silence!' (Biggles was the hero of a popular series of boys' books.)

We were given a book of manners. This consisted of 246 rules or admonitions that we should become familiar with. Amongst other things it said: 'It is the duty of all Catholics but especially of all priests to make the truth loveable and admirable. We have no right to lower people's opinion of our religion or our vocation by crudities of conduct or ignorance of the accepted modes of behaviour. We can be sure that Our Lord, having every perfection, was also a perfect gentleman. We should be no less.' Jesus as a gentleman was not peculiar to Catholics. All the churches strove to be 'respectable'. A prominent Church of Scotland minister, John R. Gray, argued strongly that the friends of Jesus were working class or better.

A key person at the school was the 'spiritual director'. When we arrived it was a local Aberdeen priest, Duncan Stone, naturally nicknamed Rocky. He was an abstemious, not to say scrupulous character. His severity was unsuitable for boys of our age. He was replaced by Denis O'Connell from Edinburgh, whose main interest was sports. He was remembered not for anything spiritual but for setting up a series of sports competitions within the College. He had been a runner in his day and started athletic meets with other schools in Aberdeen.

Our time and our pursuits were very controlled at Blairs, as they probably were at most boarding schools. Among my memories of schooldays was being expected to learn Church music in Latin, but I was told I couldn't sing and so was excused. Less formally, we students had a weekly ritual in the refectory of singing the countdown to the next holiday time. I remember a conversation on a parental visit about whether Christmas or Easter was the more important feast. Christmas would have won even though Easter is the climax of Christian worship. Christmas was more enjoyable because of the presents. But such celebrations were never simple: I once asked permission to buy a birthday card for my mother; the rector, who had a beautiful calligraphic script, didn't approve of spending the money. He encouraged me instead to write a letter to her, a worthwhile habit that I kept up. Our spirits remained independent to a degree: one day three of us thought we would have an adventure by skipping into Aberdeen on a free afternoon. We were spotted at the bus stop by a member of staff who offered us a lift in his car. When he discovered we were not, as he had presumed, going to the dentist, he made us walk the five miles back. (Going to the dentist was painful enough for his name to be remembered: Mr Thow.)

Academically, the school left something to be desired. I remember school inspectors visiting; one thought he would start with an easy question to a boy in the front row: 'When was the Battle of Bannockburn?' When he couldn't answer, the inspector cried 'What is your name, Scottish boy?' 'Sabatino Tedeschi' came the answer, from one of the few of Italian origin. The focus was not

really on the standard curriculum, and there was no special provision for passing the Scottish Leaving Certificate exams. We just
did our regular amount of study. One of the new 'profs', Father
Des Strain, was unimpressed by the modest academic standards
of the school. He set about putting an end to public-school-type
hooliganism and bullying. Some of those who had been kicked as
juniors were not too happy to be deprived of their senior privi-
leges. But he was right. I had never been struck at home; there was
no place for it in school.

In my final year I picked up an infection which laid me low
for 10 days. Otherwise Blairs seemed a healthy environment.
We played football in winter and cricket in summer. The nearest
swimming was in the sea, miles away, which we could only go
to on a day off. The water was freezing. Three of us were once
threatened with expulsion for swimming in a nearer loch. Sledging
in the snow was according to rank, with the senior students having
the best sledges. Only the top year were allowed bikes. There was
some quiet laughter among the juniors when in the great storm
of February 1953 the roof of the shed collapsed on top of the
bikes. In summer there was a sports day where I remember coming
second in a race to a later Abbot of Nunraw.

An important character was the grieve (farm manager), who
doubled up as the PE teacher. Each year we were dragooned into
'tattie howking' during the potato harvest. Conditions were completely primitive; it was wet and cold. The compensation was that at
the break a tractor delivered to the fields as much hot tea and sandwiches as we could consume. Food at the school was not particularly
memorable, apart from a special dinner for the Queen's Coronation
in 1953: the nuns who did the catering provided a pudding in red,
white and blue, which unfortunately proved inedible.

Another break with home life happened when I forgot my
ration book, resulting in a change of name. When the book was
posted up the priest in charge took some fun in reading out the
name on it: William J. Slavin. From then on I was no longer 'John'
but Willie. (Later, in Bangladesh, none of these letters were in the
Bengali alphabet but there was an American jeep called a *Willys*,
so I became Willy.)

There was no mention of poverty at Blairs. We had no idea how
poor the poor were. It was presumed that poverty was something

people should be glad to have escaped from. Whether the government was Labour or Conservative there was a consensus that poverty did nobody any good. There was full employment. Wages crept up. Tory Prime Minister Harold Macmillan was about to tell us all that we had never had it so good. Both my sister and brother went to fee-paying secondary schools. There was definitely a belief that the harder you worked, the further you got on. I remember visiting relatives of my mother who lived in Lanarkshire. There was a feeling that her family had 'sold the jerseys' by moving to the big city. Everyone was on the up and up and we were in the vanguard.

DNA was discovered and a vaccine for polio found. Cancer overtook TB as the most common disease. Mount Everest was conquered but in South Africa apartheid was reinforced. My first political awakening was the fall of Dien Bien Phu in 1954. Having recovered from their defeat in the First Indochina War the French were trying to hold onto their empire in Indochina. The newspaper headline was that they had been overrun by the 'Yellow Peril'. Even then I suspected this was not the whole story. I might have been inclined to communism with a small c, while remaining Catholic with a large C.

17

La Dolce Vita

The Holy City gave me my first sight of how ill-divided the world was. In Rome there was wealth in the Church. Pope Pius XII was carried by footmen on an elevated chair and surrounded by nobility. He was Pontifex Maximus with a triple tiara. We lived opposite the Anglo-American Hotel, which was busy with well-heeled tourists. Round the corner was the beginning of the Via Veneto, where we could see the likes of Sophia Loren having coffee at a pavement café. Although the decolonisation process had begun and guerrilla war had broken out in what would become known as the Third World, there were as yet no calls for revolution among the students of the Scots College. There were debates in the College where some argued that the Church required a stable state. This sounded like fascism to others. The film *La Dolce Vita* became shorthand for the effects of opulence.

Togliatti's Communist Party was pressing the ruling Christian Democrats hard. Most of us had been brought up working class. We weren't part of the establishment but we wanted to be part of the Church. When I am asked where I was trained I find it difficult to reply. In Rome the emphasis was entirely on the academic. There was no professional training designed for clergy as such. It was more like an initiation process into hitherto secret codes, possibly a bit like joining the Masonic Order.

The Pontifical Scots College, founded in Rome in 1600, had had a chequered history. There was still a memorial Mass for the repose of the soul of Bonnie Prince Charlie. It was only 12 years since the end of World War Two and the regime of the College was Spartan. Apparently it was worse in Paris, where the Scottish students at Saint Sulpice told us they were still eating all their food out of one bowl. My father had told me to be careful of drinking water 'on the Continent'. The Scots College had a fountain with water piped in from the Alban Hills through a viaduct built by one of the popes in the sixteenth century. Santa Claus had not yet arrived from America. Presents were given on the Epiphany, 6 January, the feast of 'La Befana'. The traffic policeman in the nearby Piazza Barberini was surrounded by gifts on that day.

We had no sooner arrived in Rome than we were taken by older students to a trattoria where the wine was delivered by the carafe. Having returned the worse for wear from this initiation we were upbraided by the vice rector John 'Bobo' Gogarty, who called us 'little beasts', a name that then stuck to us. 'You can take a horse to the water,' he said, 'but you can't make it drink!' The ironic part of this episode was that Bobo had a drink problem himself. Possibly he was trying to impress upon us how lucky we were to have been chosen to study in Rome.

We were learning to live above our station. University bursaries covered our bed and board. We had to buy our own books and pay for our uniform. We still depended on our families for support. This was easier for some than for others. I remember seeing for the first time a student eating a whole bar of chocolate by himself. It was possible to be a student for the priesthood and to be selfish. The pound sterling was strong against the Italian lira. We could afford holidays in the Dolomites, the Adriatic Coast and even in Capri. We were able to supplement our frugal food provision by going to the local shops. We each kept a little paraffin stove in our rooms for tea or coffee with pastries. When a student in the North American College tried this he was upbraided by the rector (later Archbishop of New York) for 'eating cookies in the Red Belt'. Central Italy was considered to be full of 'commies'.

Poverty was thought to be a special calling for those who were studying for religious orders like Franciscans and Dominicans. They wore sandals and no socks but some had cameras round their necks. We once met a Jesuit professor who had forgotten to draw money for his bus fare but would only accept help from us if we promised to get it back the next day from his bursar. We visited the Camaldoli monastery at Frascati. I saw the meals being delivered to the monks. It looked like leftover peelings. Then we saw the graveyard: 88, 89, 92 years old, etc. Food from the garden was clearly good for you!

Day trips (*gitas*) were great occasions for us. We went to the cathedrals at Orvieto and Montepulciano, places famous for their wine. Once a year Sir Anthony Cheke from the British embassy led us to the top of Rocca di Papa to see the sunrise. We were invited to the embassy for occasions such as the visit of the Queen. We had Mass in the Vatican with the Pope. Our main contact with the Vatican, however, was to delegate a student to buy duty-free cigarettes for the students who smoked. The designated 'Cigarette Man' held an important office amongst us. He was expected to maintain black-market contacts. Although I didn't smoke we were encouraged to indulge in a free cigarette on special occasions. The link between smoking and cancer had only just been detected.

The practice sermons that were prepared monthly by the students revealed that 'materialism' was thought to be not all bad. Once 'super-natural' Revelation had been accepted, common sense was good enough to see us through life's problems. A visiting Australian priest told us not to worry about preparing sermons. The last thing, he said, Catholics did before going to church was to hang their brains on the clothesline to give them an airing because they wouldn't need them in church.

By the time the Second Vatican Council started the Scottish bishops had decided to build a new college in the Holy City. The Catholic Church was growing everywhere. In Rome national colleges and congregations were expanding their facilities, though not the English College. '*Gli Inglesi*' (the English) were intent on keeping the building associated with the Reformation Martyrs even if it was in a rundown part of Rome. The Scots thought they needed more room and there was no space to develop its city-centre site. We would have to move outside the city. In retrospect it was like the end of empire where those in charge, as in Delhi in India, didn't know what to do. So they built bigger.

One year I was asked to write the year's diary for the College magazine. After it was published I happened to have broken my knee playing football against the Irish College. I was confined to my room with my leg in plaster propped up on a chair. Rector Clapperton, known for his plain speaking, visited me and upbraided me for not starting the diary with the elevation to Cardinal of the Sacred Rota judge Monsignor Heard, the first Scot so honoured since the Reformation. I had recorded it in the middle of the year when it had happened. The rector left without saying anything about my leg being in plaster. Even this honest priest was not immune from ecclesiastical snobbery.

I also got the job of being the '*falegname*' or odd-job man who was expected to report anything in need of repair. It wasn't a prestige job like sacristan, which was given to the more upright.

For the final four years of divinity we were joined by two English students coming from further studies at Ushaw College in the north of England near Durham. One of them, walking back from the Greg one day, impressed upon me that 'grace' wasn't a thing that adhered to your 'soul'. It was your relationship with God: a vivid thought. Amongst us was a Cambridge graduate and convert to Catholicism who produced plays at the summer villa such as Shakespeare's *Julius Caesar* and Jean Anouilh's *Antigone*.

It was the custom in summer that former students would visit the College. They seemed mostly to be the ones who had romantic memories of their time in Rome. The most famous alumnus of the Scots College was Frederick Rolfe (aka Baron Corvo), author of the Roman novel *Hadrian the Seventh*. He recorded that the only thing he would eat in the Scots College was a boiled egg because it was the only thing the cook hadn't touched with his hands! A perhaps more elevated literary connection of the College lies in its song, which was written by John Gray, known to some as Canon Gray of Morningside. Others knew Gray as the erstwhile friend of Oscar Wilde. Not many who knew the Canon realised he was the inspiration for *The Picture of Dorian Gray*. Not many who knew Wilde were aware his friend had become a Catholic priest.

On our first journey back to Scotland we sailed on the Rhine to the Netherlands. One of our newly ordained students, Father Moffat, had a brother who was killed in World War Two while returning from a bombing raid over Germany. He had been buried in Schoonhoven in the Netherlands. Father Moffat was the first priest, he was told, to have stayed in that Protestant village. It seemed an old-fashioned country; there were still wooden clogs outside the door. When we arrived in Scotland everyone was watching Rome hosting the Olympic Games. Two years later, on another journey home, we had the opportunity to visit East Germany, where we were able to see what poverty really looked like, with women sweeping the streets with brooms.

In 1964 my family made a great financial sacrifice to come out to my ordination by car, with my brother-in-law driving. After the service we had lunch in the College, where in my speech I was able to quote the scriptural passage for the day, which was from Jeremiah: 'I am a young man, I do not know what to say.' We were given a week off from studies and I went with the family to Assisi. St Francis, of course, declined to be ordained a priest knowing the temptations that came with it.

We students left Rome aware that there might be tensions around obedience. We were also aware of changing sexual mores. There was, however, still no teaching about poverty. The domestic staff, who were boys from one of the poorest parts of Italy, were called 'servants'. They were poorly paid but this was not something we took an interest in. We knew poverty existed in 'the Third World'. We had no idea this might present a challenge in parishes in Scotland. In particular we assumed the clerical lifestyle was something that we could look forward to. Despite the visit to Assisi it didn't occur to me that there might be a conflict between clerical comfort and the imitation of Christ.

Differences of view among the students were seen as arguments about values and not encouraged. We were not as liberal as we thought we were, particularly with respect to wealth and poverty. The Age of Empire was coming to an end. Countries were engaged in a struggle to be independent. The Cold War divided nations into the haves and the have-nots. Yet within each state there were divisions among those who had more than they needed and those who had not enough. As students in Rome we were oblivious to the looming importance of this.

A report on the state of housing in Glasgow around this time stated that 40 per cent of it should be demolished. The Resale Prices Act came into effect. The first Tesco appeared with the American mantra: 'pile 'em high, sell 'em cheap'. Package tours to 'the Continent' started. The Beeching Report cut the railways down to size. The space-age race between the USSR and the USA was on. Russia sent a dog called Laika into space. We had a hymn (to Our Lady): 'Here in an orbit of shadow and sadness, veiling thy splendour thy course thou hast run.' It led to the irreverent thought – poor little Laika! The election of John F. Kennedy as the first Catholic president of the USA impressed us greatly. Like many

I remember where I was when one of the students came to tell us he had been assassinated.

In summer 1963, our final summer in Rome, one of my fellow students, Des McAllister, and I joined eight students from Drygrange, the Edinburgh seminary, on a visit in a rickety van to the Holy Land. Among my recollections were the wrecked vehicles along the vast Turkish plain, left there, we were told, as a warning to reckless drivers. Syria was the most difficult country to travel in, with checkpoints everywhere, some of them illegal and one trying to get us to buy snacks. Since it was before the 1967 war when Israel took over most of the West Bank we were able to visit all the main pilgrimage sights. Visiting an Arab refugee camp, we were shown fields which had been Arab but were now within Israel. 'Don't worry,' we were told, 'we'll get those back.' Clearly not. On the return journey we tried to change some Bulgarian money in Yugoslavia and were laughed at. Yugoslavia had distanced itself from the Soviet bloc.

I had taken an optional course on the subject of 'worker priests' in France who had been revived after World War Two. The figure who caught my imagination was Abbé Pierre. He was a priest in Lyons from a well-off background who had taken part in the Resistance with the son of Charles de Gaulle. After the war he had become an MP. He was then beseeched by the poor to help them. His response was that France had just fought a war against Germany. Could it not fight a war against poverty? He became known as the priest of *les charbonniers* (the charcoal burners). He took them out to the city dumps (and there could not have been much dumped in Paris at that time) to recycle whatever they could salvage. When a mother and child froze to death in winter he made an impassioned plea for better housing. He then set up communities where the poor could help each other. To these he gave the name 'Emmaus', from the story in the Gospel where after his death Jesus told two of his followers not to despair. Emmaus became in France the equivalent of the Salvation Army in the UK. Abbé Pierre, with his commitment to the poor, offered me a personal model for how to be a priest.

18

West End

The year I was ordained in Rome, 1964, Pier Paolo Pasolini produced in the poverty-stricken south of Italy *Il Vangelo secondo Matteo* (The Gospel According to Matthew). Pasolini was a Marxist who wanted to strip back the teaching of Jesus to its essentials. We had a regular film show in the Scots College but we didn't show Pasolini's film. Instead of being seen as a useful corrective it was seen as Communist polemic. We didn't see Jesus as Pasolini saw him, a *poverello* (Little Poor Man) like St Francis of Assisi. For us, Jesus was still the gentleman of seminary teaching.

Toryglen, my first appointment as a priest that same year, was anything but Tory. Many of the Irish clergy performed heroics on behalf of the poor in Glasgow, but they had received in Ireland an even more limited education than I had got in Rome. A better education was already available to many of their parishioners. Some clergy were too slow to get out of the habit of speaking down to people. It was said that in some parishes the only Catholics who voted Tory were the clergy.

It would be hard to find a bigger contrast between my brief initiation in Toryglen and my home for the next five years. Broomhill was entirely middle class, with a very small number of Catholics. The Dutch owners of the department store C&A had wanted a private school in the West End for the children of their Catholic managers. The archdiocese agreed to build a church small enough not to offend the Presbyterian neighbours. Land was acquired in the name of a third party from the eccentric A.E. Pickard. When he heard it was the Catholic Church that had bought it he told his lawyers to cancel the sale, but they said it was no longer his. Buying the property and building the church and presbytery cost, in the 1960s, just less than £100,000. It was to be called Our Lady of Perpetual Succour, Broomhill. At the same time the archdiocese was opening another church, Our Lady of Good Counsel, Broompark. There was a regular mix-up of mail. The diocese didn't concern itself with such petty things.

Father Pat Smith, the priest appointed to manage the new parish, had been the chaplain in Barlinnie, Scotland's biggest prison. Not long before his new appointment he had been required to assist one of the last prisoners executed in Scotland, the mass murderer Peter Manuel. Whatever it did to Manuel, it was clear that capital punishment hadn't done Pat Smith any good. He was distinctly nervous. He had been an assistant to Canon McBrearty in Springburn, who my parents had held in high regard when they lived there. Pat told me some less endearing stories about him. A petrol station was opened on the spare ground next to the church. Some parishioners thought this a bit infra dig. It became busier than the church – an interesting sign of the times.

At Blairs I had been told I would never be able to speak in public – I'm not sure why; possibly I was too shy. Perversely, this turned out to be the spur that I needed. I took up the mantra popular with African-American preachers: read yourself full, think yourself clear, speak yourself hot. Catholic priests were not expected to discourse at length as in other denominations. They had, however, just acquired an invaluable asset. The new lectionary for Mass in English was based on a three-year cycle of the first three Gospels (with the Fourth Gospel in Lent and Easter). This made it possible in sermons to address just one idea from the appointed Gospel passage. A topical introduction with a reference to how the passage affected Christians in the past allowed an application to contemporary life. I was described as speaking to the point.

An obvious criticism of parish life was the lack of anything like an annual audit of the congregation. Preaching on the Temptations of Christ it could be said that Jesus rejected miracles, mysteries and authority. Yet the Church depended on all three. An audit would have shown that the Catholic Church in Scotland was moving towards an imitation of the more established churches in the country. It was doing better among the well-off than it was doing among the poor. Many of the great parishes of the past were being depopulated. Some families were buying a house for the first time. Others were getting an indoor toilet and a hot water supply in new local authority housing. But there were yet others who were being left behind, like those in the remaining riverside slums.

There weren't many middle-class Catholic families in Glasgow in the 1960s, so to make up the numbers our parish boundary was extended to include some of these old tenements. Visiting them was a bit of a revelation for someone like me, who had been brought up among the skilled working class. There were families who at times ran out of money for gas and electricity. I took to illustrating my sermons with reference to the poor in our midst.

Most of the parishioners were aware of deprivation because their families had been in a similar situation only a generation or two before, and I was getting a truer picture of it myself. One of them, the gentile partner in a Jewish firm, introduced me to the Simon Community. The name was taken from Simon of Cyrene, who helped Jesus carry his cross. It was founded by Anton Clifford-Wallich following some of the ideas of Dorothy Day of the American Catholic Worker movement. Some parishioners took part in a weekly soup kitchen in the city centre. I also went to hear Padre Borelli, the priest of the *scugnizzi* (street children) in Naples. The nun in charge of the private school established within our parish insisted on taking in children who had 'special needs', which was not appreciated by all the fee-paying parents. But things were changing: comprehensive education had just started. The city council, with its large complement of Catholic councillors, put a Catholic comprehensive school in the middle of Jordanhill, which was full of people who owned their houses and attended the local churches. The pupils were bussed into the West End from the outlying housing 'schemes'.

There was no encouragement to put into practice any of the ideas that had been raised during my student days in Rome about 'worker priests' – a French movement of the 1950s, where priests worked in factories during the week. By 1965 I was a student at university and had acquired a little car, a Mini, with the special allowance I got. Most of my contact with the archdiocese was about money. They regularly managed to forget to send my allowance to attend university. I remember once saying to my mother that I had to get back to work. She looked at my hands and said: 'Son, you have never worked.' I think she was quite pleased that one of her children had not entered the rat race.

One big influence on me was contact with clergy from other denominations, for example when we cooperated through Christian Aid door collections. I also got the chance to visit the Iona Community's house in Clyde Street, where Church of Scotland volunteers worked with the homeless. One of the local ministers had been a well-known Scottish cricketer. Ministers were not well-off and had to maintain families as well. They could have had good jobs but accepted the impoverishment that came with working for the Church. In comparison I had it easy as a bachelor.

Two experiences with money are worth recording. In 1967 I went to the States for the first time to visit my uncle, aunt and cousin on Long Island near New York. Through a former classmate from the North American College in Rome I arranged to spend a month in a nearby parish to see something of the American church. I was amazed at the money flowing around. There was a secretary who dispensed 'stole fees', i.e. offerings for baptisms, marriages and funerals. This was in addition to the donations for daily Mass. I was even given a fee for filling in for one of the priests for the month. It was very business-minded. I returned with a fistful of dollars. I had the feeling that, as the Gospel says, I had received without charge, I should have given without charge. I was surprised, not to say a little scandalised, by this intrusion of capitalism into the Church. Clergy were entitled to bed and board. But the visit raised questions about the propriety of taking money for religious services. The parish priest in Central Islip in New York was Irish-American and a racist. When he dropped me back at my uncle's house he said: 'Willy, you are the first Communist I have ever spoken to.'

The other experience was, in 1969, a month in Russia, then part of the USSR. On the buses in Moscow there was an honesty box to take the fares. The older people all paid. Most of the younger ones didn't bother. On a busy bus I observed the older people trying to stretch for the box and the younger ones taking the money and putting it in the box for them and going on with their conversation unperturbed. From that scene alone it was clear that the Communist system wasn't going to survive. On entering Russia by car from Finland we were hours at the border while our vehicle was searched. We were hardly on our way when we were approached by men in motorbikes wanting to buy our

Western clothes. On our way back through Prague we saw graffiti everywhere saying 4–3, the score by which the Czechs had beaten Russia in the World Ice Hockey Championships. Within 20 years the system had imploded.

Not all the members of the church in Broomhill approved of my version of the 'social gospel', even if the implication was socialisation rather than socialism. Some parishioners were not happy to hear constant harping on about what the Gospel said about wealth and poverty. To everyone's surprise it was not me but the parish priest who was moved. This was presumably for not keeping me in check. In 1969 the archbishop sent for me, saying he had heard I talked a lot about the poor. I thought this was a commendation. He then said he was going to send me to live among the poor, which came as something of a shock.

I did have some sense of my own importance and how I might be more effective with the better-off. At that stage it was still possible that the priesthood might have become a career for me, rather than a calling, and I would have gone on to 'do well' in the Church. The decision to send me to a 'poor parish' probably had little to do with the archbishop himself. The assistant bishop was in touch with the better-off members of the parish. Before I left I was invited to speak to the Catenians, a group of Catholic businessmen. As the topic was 'the priest as professional' I wore my university tie in place of a Roman collar. I was asked if I still considered myself a Catholic.

The Peter Principle says that if you haven't reached the next level in your profession within five years, you are unlikely ever to do so. If you have achieved it, why stay on? The archbishop's command was a turning point in my life. If he had not thought of sending me away from the well-off to a ministry among the deprived my life would have been different. From then on, as it happened, my life began to work out mostly in 'five-year plans'. Most of these ministries, one way or another, were directed towards a service to the less fortunate.

19

East End

When I went to Parkhead in 1970 St Michael's Church was still the old one in Salamanca Street, which was next to a coffin factory. The enormous new one turned out to be a white elephant. The locals called it the 'Taj Mihol' (Gaelic for Michael). There had been extensive demolition and the people had been moved out of Parkhead to the peripheral schemes. Some who couldn't cope with the lack of amenities crept back to the East End. The presbytery was only a year old yet where the previous priest had taken down his pictures you could see the original colour of the wallpaper. The rest was covered in a thin layer of red dust from Parkhead Forge, which had once employed over 20,000. The priest I was replacing had been removed to Ireland because he had knocked down a boy and was suspected of drink-driving. That was what happened in those days.

The worst area was the incongruously named Palace Street. One day a girl from there came to say they had nothing to eat because their (single) mother had been imprisoned for not sending the oldest girl to school. I gave the girl money to get fish suppers for their evening meal. As I sat in a broken chair in their home, one of the smaller ones told me to look at her wee brother. She said to me: 'He's peed on his chips!' Visiting homes was a privilege but also an eye-opener. It was the first time I saw unemployed men at home during the day. The women worked in the local Irn-Bru factory, deafening work as the bottles clanked along. They had to bend down and cup their ears to hear their children at interval time. After decimalisation, introduced in 1971, they still spoke about 'ten bob bits' for the new 50p coin. There was little social agitation. During the Tory Government's 'three-day week' in early 1974, everyone came to the chapel for candles to use during the power cuts.

The worst housing I ever saw was next to Glasgow Cross. It was called, appropriately enough, Schipka Pass from an incident in the Crimean War. It was a battle zone. Who were the gangsters, I wondered? Every day I walked to school through Barrowfield, a small deprived scheme which impressed upon me the links between poverty and injustice. It had a dual carriageway through it, although nobody owned a car. Car owners from the better suburbs used it as a shortcut. Because one side was blocked off they had to drive down the wrong side of the road. Coming from the West to the East End people seemed to get smaller and walk closer to the wall after they passed the dividing line of the Heilan' Man's Umbrella (the Central Station Bridge).

Not long before decimalisation, in 1969, the voting age came down to 18 and the school leaving age was raised to 16. The less able children attended the last junior secondary in Glasgow, St Mary's. At that time school attendance in Glasgow was in the high 90 per cent. In St Mary's it was below 70 per cent. This astounded the principal psychologist. One of the staff told me that there had been a blitz of attendance officers in the area to improve this but, as he put it, 'St Mary's stood firm!' I once observed a boy coming to school in worn football boots. Apart from truancy, there were all sorts of social and psychological problems.

There were boys who struggled with 'the cat sat on the mat'. As the school psychologist I was able to test the reading ability of the whole of the first year, 300 pupils. I picked out 10 boys who probably had learned to read at one time but had mostly forgotten. They were taken out of class for special tuition using a system called *ita*. This had a simplified spelling method. The boys liked it. Some read ahead of the others to see how the story ended. Girls seemed to have paid more attention in primary school. One who was offered support begged not to be taken out of class, promising she would improve herself. Some time later her mother thanked me for teaching her to read. Much later in life I came across the two worst boys in reading ability. Both had had jobs all their life, thanks to the extra tuition.

The school found accommodation for my psychology work in the offices of the former William Arroll Engineering across the road. Apart from individual cases I was able to take on groups of pupils who were unable to cope with regular classes. The premises were visited by Colin Ward, who praised our efforts in his book *The Child in the City*. There was a Free School nearby that was being run along the lines that were being advocated at the time, which were to set up separate arrangements. I visited it but it seemed to me important to keep young people as much as possible alongside their peers. I was influenced by *Letter to a Teacher* from the alternative school in Barbiana, Italy, which had just been published. The local Child Guidance Clinic appreciated my work. The principal psychologist wrote that more intensive tuition within the school premises was a valuable initiative. We got a write-up in the *Times Educational Supplement*.

We got money to take the most deprived away for a fortnight's camp each year. It was hard work to get the most needy to come. Only once did we have to send anyone away. Fortunately the incident occurred during a visit by a councillor and the pupil was happy enough to go home in the council Daimler. Once, when I was trying to get the kids off Aberdeen beach, one girl yelled across the sands: 'Father Slavin, someone stole my knickers!' Highlights were visits to Iona with 10 difficult boys. Their visits coincided with those from an English public school. Apart from having to translate between the two groups, all went well. Our boys were always trying to steal some famous Iona doves for the 'dookits' (dovecotes) back home.

St Mary's had been promised a new site. I had acquired sufficient status to be able to point out to the authorities that it was time to end the anomaly of a junior secondary. The new site could serve all the boys of the East End. The nuns, led by the formidable Mother Felicitas, were open to change. The Brothers, led by the politically minded Brother Gall, were not. The result was a successful amalgamation with the girls of Our Lady and St Francis (Charlotte Street), while one of the St Mary's boys burnt down the Brothers' St Mungo's Academy. I thought of the prophet Nahum, when the Lord says 'I will burn your chariots in the smoke' (Nahum 2:13). When St Mary's finally closed we had a Mass which ended with 'The Battle Hymn of the Republic'. The parish priest, ensconced in his room, said he thought the revolution had started.

During the Parkhead years I was also required to visit Belvidere Hospital on the banks of the River Clyde. It had been the old fever hospital, where I had spent time as a child. It still had wards for TB, where the patients slept outside in summer. They all had poor backgrounds. I was once asked by them if I could intercede with the authorities to get them back inside before winter – the authorities agreed. One sister, Sister Ward as it happens, had charge of the first frail elderly people to be brought in for nursing. She ran a model ward with the old women grouped round her nursing station. On a call one night a new young doctor confessed to us that she thought she had killed one of them with her efforts at revival. We were able to assure her she had tried her best. I was asked to preach at the hospital's centenary. I recalled the story of the first superintendent, who had diagnosed a case of bubonic plague in the East End carried by a rat from a ship. He had sealed up the house before the infection spread.

One of my father's stories was of the poor woman at Christmas singing for pennies outside the homes of the rich. When she saw their tables full of food she burst out crying, thinking of the poor child at her side. The boy said to her: 'Why are you crying, Mammy, you're singing great!' Anatole France said: 'We know the mercy of God is infinite because he has pity even on the rich.'

In the East End of Glasgow I saw the long-term effects of poverty on the health, education and welfare of people. Early learning was an obvious casualty. My psychological studies had persuaded me that deficiencies in the first six- to eighteen-month period of life were very difficult to compensate for. At the same time, it was evident that some were at least as bright and able as the better-off but never got the same chance to prosper. It was possible to believe that the kind of religion they embraced was indeed the opiate Marx accused it of being.

Poverty in a place like Glasgow was not a virtue but an injustice. However, the young people of the East End of Glasgow were gradually overcoming the dreadful conditions suffered by their forebears. Schooling enabled the children to get on. Many of the teachers, doctors and social workers took the money they got for working in poor areas and went home without thinking any more about the economic gulf between their lives and those of the poor. But some spoke up. Without thinking of becoming poor myself, I began to see that there was a place for more able people to articulate the effects of poverty on others. There is evidence that effective change occurs when the better-off use their talents on behalf of the poor.

20

Third World

Ordination in Rome had given me a sense of the worldwide Church, and I had kept in touch with priests from different parts of the world. Events around the world also influenced me: the war and resultant famine in Biafra in the late 1960s and early 1970s caught everyone's attention. Prominent among those who wanted to carve Biafra as a Catholic country out of Nigeria, separate from Animists and Muslims, were the Holy Ghost Fathers, the Killeshandra Sisters and the Marist Brothers. After Biafra's attempt to secede from Nigeria was quashed, with help from the previous colonial power (Britain), several of the religious there, including my cousin Brother Norbert, got jail sentences.

After the Vatican Council, priests were being encouraged to think of the Church in a wider sense. In the Church at large the idea of conversion had changed. Mass conversions had been part of the colonial experience. Paulo Freire, the radical Brazilian writer, had popularised the idea of 'conscientisation', that is making the poor aware of why they are poor and how they are able to change their own situation. Having attempted that in the East End of Glasgow, by 1975 I was thinking it might be possible to make a comparable contribution further east.

I didn't want to have to spend time learning another language, so the Indian subcontinent appealed. India didn't want foreigners, so through a friend who worked in the Vatican I asked about Pakistan. There was some correspondence. The first bishop to whom I wrote lost my letter. The reality was that there were plenty priests there at that time. However, the Xaverian Missionary House in Glasgow had a place in Bangladesh. I told them I had got permission to work overseas for five years if their confrères could use me.

In my diary at the time I wrote: 'As we criticise the Victorians of Kensington and Dennistoun for ignoring the poverty of Cheapside and Calton, so I believe we will all be condemned for ignoring the poverty in the other side of the global village. For through modern media we know more about Calcutta than they knew of their neighbourhood. Through the superabundance of consumer goods our young are being conditioned to things they may want but don't need. They should learn that these are provided by the sweat of workers whose wages do not feed their children. I do not believe this message can be preached unless by example. And so I go, at least for a time, to the "global Bridgeton", to experience real need, to learn from those who live there and, please God, one day to return to enable people here to live more freely.'

To help me to acclimatise I stopped off for a week in Cairo. A Scottish Sister had joined the Carmelite Convent there. She arranged for me to stay with the Carmelite Fathers in Shubra, an area of the city where religious services were available in Coptic, Arabic, French and Latin. The pyramids and the Sphinx, reached by bus from Tahrir Square, revealed themselves as silent witnesses to the mystery that was Egypt, the source of so much of what we think of as civilisation. I went inside the Cheops Pyramid. At the city museum I commented that its contents seemed sparse. The receptionist replied that if I wanted to see more Egyptian artefacts I should go to the British Museum in London!

This was my first exposure to poverty at a mass level. It was overpowering. Cairo appeared incapable of managing its population, which had been swollen by war with Israel. Islam had been strengthened by the struggle with Zionism. A sense of Arabic brotherhood had been reinforced. However, the former president, Nasser, had turned out not to be the pharaoh the country needed.

I then flew on to have a week in Bombay (now Mumbai), 'the Gateway to India'. Bombay was better than Cairo in transport but worse in housing. Shacks occupied every free space. Men flopped down on the pavement when their day's work was done. Families cooked by the drain and hung their clothes on the lamp posts. Indira Ghandi had just declared a state of emergency. One of the Jesuits surprised me by preaching on the feast of St Vincent de Paul (patron of the poor) that we should not give money to beggars: that was only salving our own conscience without changing anything.

There were many organisations that we should become part of instead. I was able to meet up with Rev. Chris Wigglesworth, in charge of Lion Gate Kirk, who showed me some of the work they were doing with street people. The Catholic Church was big and westernised. At Mass one of the hymns was to the tune of 'Danny Boy'. The Jesuits, however, had engaged with what was called indigenisation, adapting religious practice in accord with the local culture. Hinduism was as publicly obvious in Bombay as Islam had been in Cairo.

My first taste of water in India laid me low and I spent most of the week in bed. The doctor gave me Valium, which helped get me on the plane to Bangladesh.

The new military government in Bangladesh had fixed the price of rice at a rate which a day labourer could afford. During my time there the population ceased to be destitute. The local definition of poverty was rice without salt. Ordinary people could just about afford to mix dhal (a kind of soup) or a vegetable with their rice. Sometimes they could have a bit of fish which, with all the rivers, was fortunately abundant. The European priests ate a combination of Bengali and Italian food. Later, when I was in charge of the Centre at Jessore, I was able to persuade them to have the midday Bengali meal with the students. It was good for us to try to be on the same level.

I cycled and used public transport rather than seeking to raise the money for a car or motorbike. Trains had deteriorated since *Rajer shomoy* (British times) but buses were improving, as long as you didn't mind waiting for the frequent river crossings by barge. The Dutch, with their experience of dykes, had been called in to build bridges but the tributaries of the Ganges just changed course and flowed round the new structures. In times of flooding we had to remind ourselves that Bangladesh is a flood economy. Sometimes people took risks and farmed too near the river. That produced the casualties which captured headlines at home.

Bengalis are good-looking people, with dark hair and good teeth. Although there was quite a variation of skin colour, I observed that racism was universal. They had different genetic backgrounds, and over generations some had become darker through working in the sun, some fairer by staying indoors. Poor women worked out-doors. Richer men always married fairer women – and, therefore, had fairer children. Their idea was not to be 'white'. They thought we were pink – the children, behind our backs, called us 'red monkeys'. The best colour was '*forsha*', a word which originally meant Persian (Iranian) but now meant 'fair' or golden.

My own introduction to the limits of property came at my first Christmas. I had decided wearing a watch was 'Western' and left mine on my desk. When I returned it was gone. It had been an ordination present from my parents so had sentimental meaning. I decided if someone else needed it more than me then I could embrace some of the local poverty. The poor had time stolen from them. Because they had no watches the landowners deliberately returned late to the fields to say when their time was up. The trunk I had filled in Scotland with things I thought I needed failed to arrive. So I decided to dress locally, which was simpler and more appropriate for the weather. Being poor made what you *were* more important than what you *wore*. One Christmas the local St Vincent de Paul Society got a gift of post-office uniforms from Australia and turned up at Midnight Mass proudly wearing them, impervious to the fact that Western clothes put them at odds with the rest of the congregation.

The highlight of my time with the students was an occasion when I was acting principal and it was discovered that the drains were blocked. There was the lowest caste to call upon when this happened. I suggested that the Christian faith we were teaching and learning about should be put into practice and we should get dirty ourselves. There was resistance at first but eventually all but one of the students were persuaded. I can still remember the cry of achievement when the source of the blockage was discovered. Literally amidst all the shit there was a sense of communal success. This also highlights the limitation of the adage: teach a man to fish and you feed him for a lifetime. What if he had no legal access to water? Bangladesh was still essentially a feudal society in which land (and water) was ruthlessly controlled by the few. The Mission stations had land. I impressed upon the students how important it was to make use of the land we had. We pressed every inch of our 'compound' into use.

The Xaverians did not see themselves as foreign missionaries. They had committed themselves to spending the rest of their lives in the country they were sent to. They did not feel the need to go native – dealing with the climate was enough of a trial. They gently mocked those they called 'winter pilgrims', Italian benefactors who volunteered to visit in the cooler season. Jessore turned out to be a convenient base from which to travel around the country and see in different parts a diverse approach to mission. I learned enough Bengali to be able to write a little booklet on the social implications of the Gospel.

I crossed the border to Calcutta in India several times as there was a good road from Jessore. Compared to India, the situation in Bangladesh was like South American poverty compared to the wealth of the United States. Western influence was far more obvious in Calcutta. There were skyscrapers being built with bamboo scaffolding. The underground was being carved out with so-called 'coolies' dangling from ropes. Buses were fast and trams cheap in Calcutta, although the poor rickshaw wallahs were still ubiquitous. In Park Street I visited a bookshop as good as any I had seen in the UK. Memories of the British Raj were everywhere. Public notices were in Hindi, Bengali and English. Advertising was in English. Indians from all over the subcontinent came to Calcutta with all their different languages, making English the common tongue.

The great risk for our students at Jessore was that they would imitate the teachers' Western ways. They might be tempted themselves to become '*sahib*', master. The Irish girls who worked for the Concern charity employed a man to do their laundry. Our own bishop was less than impressed when one of the priests made a chalice for Mass out of a coconut. We got a public holiday on the death of Chairman Mao, who was supposed to have eradicated poverty in China. Mao said: 'A peasant has to stand for a long time with his mouth open before a roast duck flies in.' He also said: 'I am a solitary monk who travels through the world with a leaky umbrella.'

East Bengal had produced jute and the port of Dacca (later Dhaka), Narayanganj, was called the Dundee of the East because Dundee was where much of the jute was exported to. There are several studies of how jute workers both in Bengal and Scotland were kept poor in the days of the British Empire. Technology allowed the owners to buy cheaply and sell dearly. There were also tea plantations on the border with India, many of which had been managed by Scots. Most of them remained in Assam in India after Partition but it was possible to visit some on the Bangladesh side. I often wondered why tea was so cheap in comparison to whisky, since both were mostly water and both allegedly addictive. I have heard (Scottish) women say they would murder for a cup of (Indian) tea.

I read Dickens' *Bleak House*, with its story of the effects of smallpox. The signs of the infection were on the faces of those around me. Infection in general in Bangladesh produced a rate of infant mortality comparable to that of Glasgow a century earlier. I had only one serious health problem in Bangladesh. An infection went through a group of students and I ended up with herpes in one eye. It can whiten the pupil and I remember the pain as that of the damned. As it happened our own doctor was in the USA but I was sent to the military medic at the local cantonment, who was able to contain it. That summer the papal nuncio, who was Australian, had arranged for me to have a break in Australia where I was sent to the local hospital and was treated by an ophthalmol-ogist from Glasgow! I was invited to accompany some local high school pupils to a film. They ate more at the cinema than a village in Bangladesh might eat in a day. Visiting their school I told the pupils I had come to Australia to bring one million Bengalis into an empty part of their country. They protested noisily. I said that they wouldn't be convicts of course. That didn't help. One girl stood against the rest and supported the idea. I also got to visit Canberra and Melbourne, where I met a relative who was a priest working with the homeless.

There was the story of a poor missionary who was once offered by a rich man all the money he needed if only he would baptise the rich man's dog. After resisting for a long time eventually he gave in because he needed money so much. The rich man built a church, a school and a dispensary for the poor. When the bishop heard about it he scolded the priest. But then there was an earth-quake and the bishop's cathedral was destroyed. He came to see the poor priest to ask if the dog needed to be confirmed by the bishop. The Jesuit Provincial, Michael Campbell-Johnson put it like this: 'The needs of the poor should be before the wants of the rich; the freedom of the weak before the liberty of the strong; participation for all before preservation for some.' The West did not so much care about feeding more people as feeding more to those who already had plenty.

It did not seem to me that the Church in Bangladesh was at all able to intervene at a secular level. The Church at home could be criticised for the same reason. There was talk of 'rice Christians', meaning people had become Christian for material reasons. But the Church anywhere usually works by providing health, education and social welfare. We had been brought up in Europe to think of our culture as Christian. We had also benefited materially. Sydney Goodsir Smith in a poem of himself lying about in bed captures well the double-edged benefits of being brought up with the benefits of socialism: 'O michty Stalin in the East / could you but see me now / the type, the endpoint, the final bloom / of decadent capitalistical thraldom.'

Europe had retained only nominal religious faith but the benefits of the Judaeo-Christian inheritance remained. When Mahatma Gandhi was asked what he thought of European civilisation he said he thought it would be a good idea. We learned that we were not the paragons of virtue we had been brought up to believe we were. Ghandi adopted the Jain ideal of *ahimsa*. This is a Sanskrit term sometimes translated as the absence of hatred. But Gandhi saw it as much more. He used the illustration of everyone pushing to get to the one narrow ticket window first. If they took their time everyone would be served.

When I did return to Scotland after five years I still had some time to run on my visa and so I returned to Bangladesh for a final visit at Christmas. The media picked this up and put me on the front page as turning my back on Western glitter. This was only partly true. I found Christmas among the poor more enjoyable than among my own. However, many years later Cardinal Winning said it had been a serious misjudgment. It was one thing to embrace the poor but there was no need to criticise the better-off. This reminded me of the story of an American priest who worked overseas. The bishop thought to recognise him by making him a monsignor. The priest was horrified and refused. The bishop insisted, saying it was not just for him but for others too. 'Think how pleased your mother would be,' he said. 'Make my mother a monsignor,' the priest replied. We were supposed to help the poor without offending the rich.

21

Justice or Peace?

I returned from Bangladesh to the Britain depicted in *Cathy Come Home*, Ken Loach's 1966 film about homelessness. The chair of a Housing Association in the West End of Glasgow, a friend and a Church of Scotland minister, had some flats in Byres Road that had been acquired for social housing. He was sure it would be some time before the money was available to modernise them. Essentially, they were available for squatting. With others who were interested in a simpler lifestyle – a family of four, an unemployed man and myself – it was possible to live there rent-free. We learned to heat ourselves (by wearing extra sweaters) instead of heating the building we lived in. The real cold came from the climate being created by Thatcherism.

After two years of this, the Sisters of the Assumption offered us two flats they were giving up in Ruchill – a small, hard to let housing scheme to the north of the city. Those of us who took up the offer – a new group of single people – took as our model of living the New York Catholic Worker houses where hospitality to the poor was practised. We also took on their Friday night custom of meetings open to others 'for clarification of thought'. Many visitors got their first impression of the Church's involvement in social action on those occasions. We used 'Campaign Coffee' which didn't taste so nice but sent some money back to the producers. Alasdair Gray called it Sandinista Coffee after the revolutionary movement in Nicaragua.

What had brought me back from Bangladesh was an invitation to help establish the new Catholic Justice and Peace Commission for the Scottish bishops. This had been one of the initiatives that followed the Second Vatican Council. It was already active in a number of countries. Archbishop Winning had been in charge of the fledgeling Justice and Peace Commission but it didn't suit his temperament to have lay people speaking in the Church's name. He was succeeded by Bishop Jim Monaghan, auxiliary in Edinburgh, who came from a Young Christian Workers background. Their motto was: see, judge, act. This fitted in better with the vision of Father Bob Bradley, who had started up the movement in Scotland. A room was rented from the Jesuits in the centre of Glasgow, as an office and a meeting place.

Other churches had effective peace movements following on from earlier anti-nuclear protests focused on nuclear submarines in the Holy Loch and Faslane. I saw my job as being to get Catholics to understand the importance of politics for their faith. We took Bishop Monaghan to meet the Scottish leaders of the miners' strike. No Church in Scotland, however, followed the example of the Dean of Durham, who collected money in his Church for the strikers. I quickly made the acquaintance of others in the field, like Rev. John McIndoe of the Kirk's Church and Nation committee. There was also Hugh Bain of Scottish Churches House, Danus Skene of Scottish Churches and World Development (SCAWD), Paul Baker of Scottish Education and Development (SEAD) and Helen Steven of the Iona Community.

Anne Forbes in Leeds was regarded as having the template for Justice and Peace work in the UK. She introduced me to Paul Rogers of Bradford University Peace Studies department and John Battle, the future MP and minister. There was also the Catholic Institute for International Relations (CIIR) and Pax Christi, the international peace movement. In Ireland there was Jerome Connolly of Trócaire, the Irish Church's Development Agency. I visited them in Northern Ireland and stayed in the Passionist House in the Ardoyne. I thought they had switched on the washing machine during the night. They said it was British Army helicopters checking their bins. Some Catholic women told me that, if it had been bad before, it got much worse when the guns came out.

I flew to the USA to catch up with contacts I had made in Bangladesh. These were members of Maryknoll, the main American Catholic foreign mission centre. There I met Gustavo Gutiérrez, the founder of Liberation Theology. This had been started in South America mostly by Basque priests working among oppressed peasants. In New York there was Father Ed de la Torre, who had just been released from prison in the Philippines. In Canada I was at a Mass celebrated by Cardinal Léger, who had resigned his archbishopric in Montreal in order to live in a leper colony in Africa. As at Vatican Two the French-Canadian speakers in Peace and Development groups had a more radical approach than those in English-speaking Canada.

The Scottish Justice and Peace movement certainly had sympathy for and some solidarity with the poor of the Third World. There was less understanding as to why some remained poor in our own midst. The St Vincent de Paul Society spoke about the 'deserving' poor. Catholics were on the way up the social scale but some remembered their own poorer background. That kind of poverty they now associated with overseas scenes on TV. They wanted to do something about this. The Scottish Catholic International Aid Fund (SCIAF) had been set up by two head teachers for that purpose. It was my job to try and promote a more radical approach about the causes of poverty both at home and abroad.

Luckily one of the first visitors we had was Archbishop Hélder Câmara from the poor north-east of Brazil. His famous saying was: 'When I give to the poor they call me a saint; when I ask why they are poor they call me a Communist.' Communism had lost much of its voice in Scotland after the crushing of the Hungarian revolution in 1956 and the acquisition of nuclear arms by the USSR. However, Strathclyde Region at its inauguration in 1975 had commissioned a background study to determine a programme of social renewal. It was as close as one could imagine to a policy based on Liberation Theology.

Jo Grimond MP, the leader of the Liberal Party, said money had become not only a sacred cow but the golden calf to be worshipped by the tribes of the West. The question for the churches was whether they had contact any longer with the poor. The German politician Willy Brandt, who had produced a document on international development, visited Glasgow to speak on his vision of 'One World'. Valpy Fitzgerald, an Irish economist working in the Netherlands, gave an invigorating talk on the economic facts of life. Basically, he said, if you are vulnerable economically you are vulnerable all along the line.

Among the reading I was doing at that time was Primo Levi. How, he asked, could anyone be treated as badly as the Jews had been by the Nazis? Equally challenging was Levi's survival after a long, tortuous journey back to Italy before his eventual suicide. Frantz Fanon's *Black Skin, White Masks* asked how the oppressed could be prevented from simply taking the place of their previous masters and becoming oppressors themselves. Herbert Marcuse's *One Dimensional Man* suggested a way out of dependence on slave labour with a new vision of the global village based upon technological developments.

Justice and Peace was an acquired taste. Paulo Freire's model of 'conscientisation' had served well in Bangladesh. The work of Justice and Peace required not only personal conversion but also social commitment. It was our minds that needed to be socialised. Helen Liddell, then secretary of the Scottish Labour Party, confessed herself horrified when she heard me speak in church. I was mixing religion with politics. Another 'devout Catholic' said she felt the need to go to confession because she had been leading a strike. There was in their minds a separation of politics and religion. Catholics who were involved in politics tended to keep this distinct from their church-going. I was asked to give a series of short talks for the religious slot on Radio Clyde. I was told the scripts for two of them were 'too political'.

During my time as national secretary of the Catholic Bishops' Justice and Peace Commission we enjoyed an *annus mirabilis* in 1982. First of all the Commission had a meeting of 70 lay people from all over Scotland and elected a lay chairman, Jim McManus from Dundee, setting up procedures for making Justice and Peace effective in all the parishes. In our own house in Ruchill we decided not to pay the poll tax. Instead we put the money into a fund which would allow us to respond to appeals for help.

In the same year the Commission prepared for the bishops a document on disarmament written by Bishop Conti, Father Gerry Magill of Drygrange Seminary and myself. It clearly stated that if it was immoral to use weapons of mass destruction then, according to the Gospel as distinct from realpolitik, it must be immoral to threaten to use them. Archbishop Winning and I went to Cardinal Gray, then president of the Scottish Bishops, to get his signature. The English Justice and Peace Commission was being advised by Michael Quinlan from the Ministry of Defence. Scotland was too small to cause worry in itself but the Vatican was concerned that the American bishops might be persuaded to take our line rather than the more cautious English approach. The Scottish Justice and Peace Commission provided what the war historian Liddell Hart, describing the lone opposition of Bishop Bell of Chichester to the carpet bombing of Germany in World War Two, said was 'the wider view and the longer vision'. Later, in 1984, we were invited to NATO HQ in Brussels.

Also in 1982 Pope John Paul II visited Scotland. In front of 300,000 at Mass in Bellahouston Park Justice and Peace was invited to take part in the warm-up session where it could be demon-strated that J&P was 'constitutive' of the Gospel as Pope Paul VI had proclaimed. The pro-life groups were asked to join us but they declined since they believed they should have had the main spot themselves. Mock-up Polaris missiles were carried from the youth event in Edinburgh to Glasgow and set up on the stage. There was an effort to include those who might not normally be thought about. Warm-up singers included an exile from Pinochet's Chile and Belle Stewart from the travelling people.

The Edinburgh quarterly *Cencrastus* published my reflections on the papal visit to Scotland. The editors were amazed how Scottish – and not Irish – the event had appeared; Catholicism in Scotland had been becoming less 'Irish' since the ending of mass immigration from Ireland to Scotland before the Second World War. In 1982 there were more English than Irish born in Scotland. The restoration of the Catholic Church in Scotland in the nineteenth century had been powered by priests from Enzie in Banffshire. They wanted the Catholic Church in the country to remain Scottish. One of them asked what would have happened if the Irish hadn't come; the response was that the Scottish Catholic Church 'would have been smaller – but better'.

As late as 1950 the archbishops of Edinburgh and Glasgow had been respectively a MacDonald and a Campbell. When Paisley and Motherwell were created in 1948 the first bishops were a Black and a Douglas – all very Scottish. Mixed marriages meant that the children chosen at random to have their First Communion at Bellahouston didn't have 'Catholic' (i.e. Irish) names. Even more astonishingly, the famous Lisbon Lions who won the European Cup for Celtic in 1967 didn't have a single Irish name. The MP for

Coatbridge, supposedly a Catholic enclave, had been a Protestant minister. Religious boundaries were not what they seemed to be.

The writer Tom Gallagher wrote that the combination of the Catholic Church and the Left in Scotland was unique. In the 1920s the Labour MP John Wheatley had been rebuked by his parish priest but was regarded as Labour's greatest housing minister. Yet although there were Celtic crosses at Bellahouston the official logo of the papal visit to Scotland was based on the union flag. Nationalism was seen as a preserve of the Church of Scotland. There were no non-white people at Bellahouston. The Catholic Church in Scotland was coherent but parochial. The booklet for the occasion had a touch of 'Brigadoonery' about it. There was no mention of labour history, nor of the betrayal of the clans by their Catholic chiefs.

We followed this high profile for Justice and Peace with a statement on South Africa, in collaboration with the anti-apartheid movement. Mandela had been given the Freedom of Glasgow and Archbishop Hurley from Durban in South Africa had visited. This encouraged us to look at the 'Troubles' in Northern Ireland. I made a night visit to John Hume, spokesman for civil rights. The army captain accompanying me presumed since I was Scottish I would be on his side and felt free to speak about military tactics which were quite disturbing. On the way back my accent suggested to supporters going to a Rangers match that I was a soldier and I was offered a drink. I was amazed when a policeman told them to put their Orange banners away. They quietly did so, telling me they knew Long Kesh but they didn't want to end up in Barlinnie. In Ireland Lord Mountbatten was blown up. India was appalled. He had been the last viceroy there – they had got over their objections to him. Mother Teresa's Sisters were squeezed out of Belfast for wanting to work with both sides. We were unable to provide a statement on Northern Ireland as effective as the one on South Africa.

A planned statement on unemployment by researchers for the Justice and Peace Commission had an unexpected outcome. Unemployment had been rising steadily. It was time for the Church to say something. Archbishop Winning happened to see the J&P statement on unemployment at the printers and pulled it at the last minute. It was his job, he clearly thought, and not that of some lay outfit to comment on 'sensitive' political issues that might provoke headlines. I didn't regard myself as an office boy. It was time for me to get out. Five years seemed long enough. Fortunately Sister Isobel Kilpatrick of Notre Dame had just returned from Nicaragua and was willing to take over.

My impressions of Justice and Peace were published in the Catholic weekly *The Tablet*. The difficulty was to get people to have a sense of what the Italians called *il Vietnam in cui stiamo vivendo* (the Vietnam in which we live). We were part of a world in which capitalism demanded a price, which was the poverty of the many. The obstacle was not a lack of knowledge but a natural selfishness. The ancient Greek Socrates knew that knowledge didn't produce virtue. We needed to be able to compare our own past and make links to the present of the underdeveloped world. The parishes had liturgical movements and the schools had catechetical movements but what movements were there to stimulate justice and peace? Acceptance of the status quo was a stronger factor than openness to the poverty that was a prominent feature of the Gospel.

22

Scottish Drugs Forum

A change occurred in the prison population during the decade I spent in HMP Barlinnie. In the 1960s it was fashionable among the middle class to defy convention and experiment with drugs. Hash (marijuana) had long been available. The focus then turned to pharmaceutical products. Some of these were imported from abroad, some prescribed by rogue psychiatrists. In the 1980s the poor started to get in on the act. Small-time criminals went to London to visit the private psychiatrists. Then they started breaking into their local chemists. The less well-off progressed from the legal stuff (sugar, fags and booze) through illegal use of the legal kind (stealing pills) to the illegal stuff (marijuana, heroin and cocaine). Alcohol was no longer the first drug of choice, as it had been for the previous generation.

Working at Barlinnie gave me a massive insight into poverty. The well-off had lawyers who prevented them from being at the mercy of the courts. If they happened to end up in prison they didn't stay long. Not so with the poor, who were completely dependent on 'duty' lawyers to help them. One prisoner, when he heard the police in court fabricating the account of his arrest, said: 'Christ, I nearly believed it myself'! One of my most frightening experiences was being invited to the drugs squad Christmas party and listening to the antics they got up to chasing drug users. One widow came to me traumatised. She lived opposite Shettleston police station. The drugs squad, intending to raid her neighbour, had mixed up the sides of the landing, smashed down her door and turned her house upside down. Another well-known criminal had 'got aff'(off) because the police claimed to have knocked at his door. A neighbour had actually phoned the police station when he heard their battering ram. The stash of drugs had been thrown into the canal but the officers declined to jump in after it.

During my 10 years Barlinnie became, unwittingly, the biggest drug centre in the country. The judges, who were, of course, among the better-off, believed they could eradicate this new source of pleasure for the poor. A girl from the Gorbals got eight years for an amount of heroin you could hardly see. The prisoners joked about being sentenced at the 'high' court. In 1981 Jason Ditton, from the University of Glasgow, was the first to describe heroin use in the city as an epidemic. Under the new regime in the prison following the riot in 1987 we were able to organise a drugs conference where a number of prisoners were encouraged to speak their mind. One said he would like a baseball bat. He would use it to smash up the doctor's office. Like police surgeons, prison medical staff mostly saw their job as helping the establishment rather than their patients. Drug users were expected to go cold turkey. I remember the first prisoner to come in under the influence of drugs. The staff presumed he was an alcoholic but his pals told me to get help for him. He was having the 'heeby jeebies' and was climbing the walls of his cell coming off heroin.

It was clear that penal policy in the future was going to be substantially about drugs. Some of those who knew how little help alcoholics had got in the face of the power of the licensed trade petitioned the Scottish Office to set up some drug centres in poor areas. Funds were provided for three different initiatives in Edinburgh, Aberdeen and Ayr. There was money left over which was allocated to creating a national Scottish Drugs Forum. From various parts of the country volunteers came forward to set up a coordinating group. Many of them came from an Alcoholics Anonymous (AA) background. They petitioned Archbishop Winning for help. He gave them the use of St Peter's seminary at Cardross which he had abandoned because it was in the remote countryside.

The hope was to have a central location where professionals, family and volunteers could rationalise a response to the new problem. With my background in psychology and work in the prison I was invited to apply to run it. I got the job possibly because I told the interviewers the drug scene was like trench warfare: under pressure the foot soldiers were likely to shoot the person next to them instead of aiming for the real target, which was the politicians. A sociologist, David Liddell, was offered a part-time post. He had a wife and family. It seemed reasonable that instead he would work full time and I part time. We became joint coordinators. We were fortunate to get an able secretary in Rita McClory, who ran the office. Ken Murray, who was well known as the prison officer in charge of the Special Unit in Barlinnie, agreed to become our chair. I brought my experience from Justice and Peace to bear by setting up small groups to guide policy and establish a regular newsletter.

Unfortunately the Tory Secretary of State for Scotland, Michael Forsyth, was keen on strong medicine for the poor. There was no recognition that punishment had not cured alcoholism and was going to have no effect on drug addiction. I was asked to update the government pamphlet on drugs and managed to place nicotine and alcohol in the first two chapters. I had really wanted to start with sugar but that, at the time, would have been a step too far. Although illegal drugs came from overseas there should have been no mystique about them. Most of our young people were experimenting with tranquillisers that could be got from the chemists or even their own families. That told anyone who wanted to know that the drug problem was about the poor seeking relief from their pain.

Although many knew the eradication of drugs was never going to happen, the majority went along with the mirage of a drug-free country – apart, of course, from pills, fags and booze! In the circumstances it seemed inevitable that the cure would be as bad as the disease. Prevention strategies would themselves become an industry. And so it came to be, as everyone accepted the political diktat. A few tried to withstand the pressure to conform to the official approach, like one of the civil servants, John Gilmour, and Davie Bryce of Calton Athletic. 'Brycie' managed to win the Scottish Amateur Football Cup with a team of former drug users. I remember him at training taking time out to listen to a mother. That was more important to him than winning cups.

There were genuine efforts to try and move from the punitive approach which was filling the jails. Some of it was to medicalise the problem, which did not take enough account of the social aspect. I was invited to a conference in New York about the use of methadone. The Americans were surprised our addicts could get medication on the NHS. We were surprised that in the USA before 9 a.m. methadone was only given out to those in work. None of our drug users had a job. Our psychiatrists regarded drug users as being like the blacks in America. They wanted to tranquillise them or at least make sure they didn't affect other people. Already they were concerned about the connection between drugs and HIV/AIDS. Some drug users earned money by being willing to 'bend for a friend' in Edinburgh; rent boys were more common than elsewhere at that time. This took the HIV infection to other parts of the country.

The archdiocese arranged for me to go to a conference arranged by the Vatican and attended by Queen Sophia of Spain among others. I was able to shake hands with the Pope but otherwise nothing memorable came from it. Tony Blair, while still Shadow Home Secretary, asked me if he could have breakfast with some drug users. I said I would try and keep them up since they were late bedders! I was invited to debate the legalisation of drugs at the Oxford University Union with the newly appointed government drug 'czar', Keith Hellawell. At a meeting in London with other 'experts' I met some Colombian priests who told the audience about the problems among drug barons when they celebrated their deals with Scotch whisky! That was when the violence would start, they said.

I joined the Addiction Group at Glasgow University, which had some radical views. Professor John Davies at Strathclyde University was fond of quoting Mao Tse Tung's approach. When he gained power in China there were plenty of opium dens. Mao got the opium users together and packed them off to the countryside. He said he would be back in three months. If they were not all cured he would shoot them. In three months, whether they were cured or not, they all said they were available for work, which was what Mao wanted. What employment was there for our drug users? Davies later produced a book about the competing theories of God and particle physics which he declared a draw. Chaos theory could explain but not predict the weather. Drugs introduced an element of what the playwright Sean O'Casey called 'chassis'.

Both the prison and the drug scene were heavily related to poverty. The rich could take or leave drugs. It was mostly the poor who became addicted. The solution was not necessarily to legalise drugs. But it was no answer to imprison the addicted. It was primarily a health problem. The Americans had started experimenting with 'drug courts'. Here the judge required the accused to try and deal first of all with their addiction so that they didn't need to steal. The real task was to make drug users aware of the damage they were doing to others, including their own families. They had to be encouraged to explore ways of earning their keep without depending on 'the Man' who controlled the supply of drugs.

Capitalism is based on the Protestant ethic of delayed gratification. Heaven would be time enough to get one's reward. This offered a social paradigm that didn't impress the poor. It didn't convince those involved in sport either. They needed instant success. At the time we didn't realise there was a whole industry building up behind the closed doors of athletics. When monetary prizes increased the drug market in sports became economically bigger than the trade in marijuana, heroin and cocaine combined. Drugs were also becoming popular at dance and music venues. Younger people wanted to open 'the doors of perception', hoping to see the world more clearly – or to dull their senses and not see it at all.

I decided five years was long enough to front the Scottish Drugs Forum. Before I finished I was able to make the Scottish Drugs Forum a partner with Alcohol Concern in preparing for the International Congress in Alcohol and Drugs which was held in Glasgow in 1992. I contributed a chapter to the conference book. In a conversation with Princess Anne when she visited the Congress she was quite realistic about the drugs problem. For me it was an achievement to put illegal drugs on the same programme as legal alcohol.

How difficult was it to give up a well-paid job as coordinator of the Scottish Drugs Forum, which had now acquired a certain social standing? Money is the greatest addiction of all. It seemed to me that for all the goodwill of the voluntary groups, very little effect could be observed by the statutory services upon the drug scene. It was a phenomenon with many tentacles. In Scotland it was triggered by a diet of sugar, nicotine and alcohol. Younger people saw illegal drugs as different and therefore to be experimented with. Culture, especially the transatlantic music scene, encouraged them. There was also an international aspect. The West had been exporting its drugs – nicotine, alcohol and the pharmaceuticals – around the world. Now other countries wanted in on the act and were exporting their drugs – marijuana, heroin and cocaine. Efforts by the United States to declare these illegal only made their transport more challenging. The poor died not just because of drugs but because their health was already poor.

23

'Alafonsus'

Archbishop Winning was made a cardinal because in the UK his was the principal voice in support of pro-life issues. But he is best remembered as a plain-speaking fellow who was on the side of the less well-off. Although he had to work with the 'movers and shakers' he seemed more comfortable mixing with ordinary people. By his time Catholics had made significant social progress. His hope was to harness a new energy to the Gospel message that would benefit the poor. St Alphonsus, because it was a busy church near the city centre, was seen as a place to show what the Church might do. The locals called it 'Alafonsus'. This was not poor speech. It betrayed the Gaelic origins of the first parishioners. *Alba*, the Gaelic for Scotland, is pronounced 'Alapa'. I had done a summer at Sabhal Mòr Ostaig College in Skye and gained an O level in Gaelic. I was also invited to preach in St Columba's Gaelic Church in Glasgow by a minister friend, Donald MacDonald.

Winning had taken as an advisor Father John King, who had experience of social outreach. King was an activist who had the vision of putting the Church's voluntary work with the poor on a professional basis. There was public money available for social work. King believed it needed a religious sense to make it fully effective. He had an entrepreneurial flair and wanted the Church to be able to combine Christian charity with financial acumen. Amongst other initiatives he acquired a large house in Helensburgh, Red Tower, and turned it into a professionally run drug rehabilitation facility.

St Alphonsus was an example of a church that had updated its liturgy without changing the mentality of the worshippers. Quick Masses with a folk group and Celtic players on their way to a match guaranteed a full house. Despite the money flowing into the coffers, Winning wanted a different image, but it seemed that no priest was willing to disrupt an apparently successful show. Because of my work with Justice and Peace and my 10 years in the prison service I was identified with the 'option for the poor'. King invested energy into helping me get a pastoral programme started in St Alphonsus.

The church was in the middle of 'the Barras' weekend market. This had been a Glasgow institution since the Hungry Twenties. It was the place were it was said you could get anything from an anchor to a pin. Many of the stallholders were old-fashioned Catholics and contributed generously to the church, which had been beautifully kept. I thought it significant that in the bustle that surrounded St Alphonsus it was locked except for services. My first act was to get it opened again during the day. Catholic churches had traditionally been places where people could slip in for a prayer or to light a candle. People flocked to the Barras during the weekend. Some came more to look than to buy. It was good that they could also have access to a quiet place in the church.

Strangely enough, I had first been attracted to the priesthood by a Redemptorist, the order founded by St Alphonsus. Alphonsus Liguori was a fascinating character, the John Wesley of Italy, who taught by open-air preaching and popular hymns. A nun inspired him to found an order. He had an ideal of *cortesia*, the courtesy that he expected to be shown to the poor which he impressed upon his first followers. He was severely criticised in his own time for a 'lax' attitude to hearing confession. The order's later reputation for strictness was said to be the result of meeting with northern European Protestantism. Alphonsus was made a bishop against his will and resigned after only six years. He returned to his apostolate of caring for the poor.

Despite such a patron, St Alphonsus parish didn't have meetings of the St Vincent de Paul Society, which in almost all Catholic parishes is the first port of call for those in need. There were no fewer than six homeless hostels in the vicinity of the church. Once enough volunteers had been recruited to set up an SVdP conference, permission was obtained from the various owners of the hostels for the SVdP to make weekly visits. We organised bingo sessions followed by tea and sandwiches. A food bank was built up to provide for those who came to the church for material help. It didn't bring Catholics back to services but it showed everyone, irrespective of denomination, that the Church cared.

One of the jobs I took upon myself was to visit the pubs in the parish, of which there were about 30. One of these allegedly was where Celtic FC was founded. Some of the locals complained that the football club's original constitution – whose main goal was to help the poor – had been lost in a fire. For a long time it was alleged that the club was run out of a biscuit tin with only a few families getting a share in the profits. As the Celtic brand became again more profitable a fund for good causes was resurrected by the club.

Everyone remembered a sermon that was not original to me but was borrowed from an Irish priest. On the Sunday dedicated to the Scottish Catholic International Aid Fund (SCIAF) the sermon consisted of three sentences: 'There are still children in the world who are starving. It's a fucking disgrace. You are more upset by me swearing than you are by children starving.' Hugh MacDiarmid wrote: 'I' mony an unco warl' the nicht / The lift gaes black as pitch at noon / An' sideways on their chests the heids / O' endless Christs roll doon.' The poet Roy Campbell described these lines as 'a deep perception of the tragic profundity of the Christian vision'.

We hosted a visit by the US Baptist Ray Bakke. He believed that urban ghettos were only a filter to funnel money to the better-off who work in them to 'help'. He said in the USA church attenders gave between $25 and $40. This allowed the churches to compete socially. In Europe the churches were restricted by their lack of funds. They expected the state to do social work. They saw their job as speaking in the name of the poor. In America, Bakke said, it was more important for the churches to be working on the streets than debating in the public square. He challenged us to do less preaching to others and to get more involved with the poor at street level. Our temptation had been to stay safely 'within the sanctuary'.

I had helped set up a credit union in Ruchill. Ian Fraser, the local minister in Calton, had an ambitious idea – a credit union that would cover Calton, Bridgeton and Dalmarnock, areas that were cheek-by-jowl but didn't get on with each other. Part of it was historical sectarianism, with Calton thought of as Catholic and

Bridgeton as Orange (Protestant). Our first meeting in Dalmarnock was chaired by a man wearing the regalia of Glasgow's Protestant team, Rangers FC! We had to bring on board social activists, one of whom was known as the Queen of the Calton. Her equivalent in Bridgeton had a son who would become a prominent city councillor, George Redmond. He became a key figure in the development of the credit union. On a visit to the States I had seen a credit union which had taken over a bank, complete with drive-in service. In the UK, banks were pulling out of poor areas. We were able to secure a redundant bank building at Bridgeton Cross, the centre of our area. With such an excellent facility the BCD Credit Union went from strength to strength.

An ecumenical group of us went to Liverpool for a conference on 'Jesus in the City'. Nearby was a church called St Alphonsus, which had been closed by Liverpool archdiocese because of depopulation. There was a hole in the roof. I said this was what we could expect in Glasgow if we did not get our act together. Disraeli had said that in Victorian Britain there were two nations: one owning the land, the other owning nothing. People living in housing estates had a long time ago been uprooted from the land. They felt little involvement in the national economy. Mrs Thatcher moved to remedy this by selling council-owned houses to their occupants, but this only increased the gap between owners and the rest, as what remained in council hands became less desirable.

Calton had been particularly badly affected by illegal drugs. In St Alphonsus we started a service for those who had died from overdoses and over a hundred names were read out the first year. It was said that from one primary class up to one-third had died already from their effects. There was a 'drugalogue', a language for those in the know. Drug 'experts' knew that most of what was said about the harmful effects of drugs was nonsense. Drugs were not the problem; the real issue was the poor health of the drug takers (the rich took cocaine and survived). The poorer type of drug users could be very greedy. Nobody really believed the drug problem would be eradicated, despite what the professionals liked to say. Drugs were a balm some of the poor felt entitled to, even if they couldn't handle the consequences. Families and friends wanted more sympathetic medical and social services. I became a member of the Association of Family Support Groups.

An ecumenical initiative was the Centre for Theological and Political Issues in New College, Edinburgh started by the Reverend Duncan Forrester who, when he had been working in India, wrote an authoritative commentary on the caste system. He was able to bring together a number of Scottish Church people from different backgrounds who believed that religion could do more in the public forum. They were aware that Scotland was changing. The majority were becoming better off. But there was emerging what was called a sub-class still trapped in poverty. The churches were among the few voices raised on their behalf.

Cardinal Winning started a fund to transfer some money from better-off parishes to poorer ones. Parishes in deprived areas were finding it harder to keep going. It was the better-off people who continued to go to church. There was some sense of solidarity among the parishes. But Winning's vision of engagement among different sectors of society did not take root. The gulf between rich and poor in society was obvious also in the churches.

24

Special Needs

The appointment to serve a different kind of poor arose when I started as chaplain to the Royal Hospital for Sick Children at Yorkhill. Many of the addresses were similar to those I recognised from prison. It wasn't the same families but the same areas that provided both ill-health and criminality. Crime and disease came from the same places. Were they both infectious? One difference between prison and hospital was that in prison the staff knew exactly what chaplains were supposed to do and hated us for doing it. In hospital the staff had little idea of what we were supposed to be doing but loved us anyway no matter what we did!

In Yorkhill Hospital there was an interesting exception to the poverty rule. The only diseases that were increasing were childhood cancers like leukaemia, which affected the rich and the poor alike. In my first parish the church's next-door neighbour in Broomhill had been the eminent paediatrician Dr Oman Craig, who had taken me to see the Children's Hospital. He said 'we are having no success with leukaemia but you will live to see it cured'. This had become true in almost 75 per cent of cases. In the 1980s there were six children's wards for infectious diseases in Ruchill Hospital. In Yorkhill by 2000 there was only one ward for infections and it had the fastest turnover, thanks to medical advances. The aim was to reduce childhood disease, if not to eliminate it altogether. It occurred to me that soon babies would have a chip implanted in an arm with their complete medical record updated on it.

Among the regular patients were those from next door Kelvin School for Special Needs – that is, for those with extra educational needs stemming from learning difficulties, physical disability, or emotional and behavioural problems, all of which are closely linked to poverty. The school was run by a Notre Dame Sister. They needed someone to play football – I was able to do that! At a Mass for special-needs pupils Cardinal Winning asked me why I was there. He was sharp enough but he hadn't made the connection between bad health and poverty. His press secretary, a friend of mine, died at 63 – a sobering moment. His job had been to try and get into the media stories the Church thought were fit to print and block those that were unfavourable. The stressful nature of such a job must have contributed to his heart attack.

The UN declared 1999 to be year of what they were still calling the 'elderly'. I was about to turn 60. I applied for a Churchill Fellowship to study the ageing process in the United States and Canada. When I applied I was asked by the board if I knew anything about Sir Winston. I said I knew he had been the Liberal MP for Dundee. I added that at the 1922 general election he had been told his seat was at risk from the Temperance candidate Edwin Scrymgeour. Churchill, who liked his drink, thought this was a joke. But he was told Scrymgeour was also a socialist who had support from the poor. Churchill arranged to be brought into the meeting in a wheelchair to explain his failure to pay more attention to his constituency. Hundreds in the audience sang: 'Tell us the old, old story; sing us the old, old song'. He lost his seat and went on to become a Tory MP in Manchester. It says much for the broad-mindedness of the committee that they still gave me a Fellowship. I was expected to spend the money as I thought fit, with minimum supervision. How very upper class, I thought.

My interest was the psychoneuroimmunology of ageing. There was evidence that there was a psychological difference in the response to the stresses of ageing. I started off in the University of Gainsville, Florida, which was studying not just healthy ageing but also the differences between rich and poor as they grew older. I then went to my cousin in Minneapolis, who was working in the Ebenezer graduated care-home system, a church-related voluntary organisation that offered retirement facilities to the less well-off. I followed this by a visit to the rich old in Las Vegas (where I stayed with the bishop) before pursuing a search for the poor old underneath the Los Angeles highways, where I was warned by my escort that we could be killed! Not many poor – outside the health system for veterans – lived to be old in the USA. My final visit was to the University of California at San Francisco to meet representatives of the American Association of Retired Persons (AARP), which covered a wide economic range. I finished the trip in Ottawa looking at the effect on ageing of the UK–style Canadian health system, where the poor had a better chance of ageing healthily.

The conclusion was that the many ills we attributed to old age had nothing to do with ageing at all. In the USA there were many in their 70s who were perfectly healthy. They were adjusting to their environment so that they could continue to look after themselves. What is seen as an ever-increasing burden of the 'elderly' on the NHS is therefore misplaced. On the one hand people do need to be encouraged to take better care of themselves. The NHS was not originally designed as a benefit system for people who have not done that. On the other hand steps need to be taken to encourage older people to remain active. It is well known that if older people keep doing things, not least for others, then that is good for their health. Bad health in the old is often a social issue and a consequence of poor economic opportunity.

Age Concern Scotland was more a policy than a grass-roots organisation. I was invited to join the board. This offered an excellent insight into the workings of a major voluntary organisation. It had acquired a chief executive who ran it with the treasurer and didn't expect much from her board. There was pressure – apparently from Prince Charles, no less, who was patron of both – to amalgamate the two leading age-related charities, Age Concern and Help the Aged. This was achieved after protracted negotiations and a new chief executive was appointed who was more responsive to grass-roots needs. At a conference on 'bed blocking' by older patients I was asked if as a priest I should not be more interested in administering the last rites. It was interesting to see what people thought the job of a priest should be. At Age Concern they did not welcome my questioning of what I regarded as an unhealthy dependence on legacies.

Glasgow Old People's Welfare Society had for a long time worked with self-help groups of older people. I was asked to sound out the possibilities of cooperation with Age Concern Scotland but they were too different as organisations. I was invited to represent ACS on the Scottish Pensioners' Forum. This was a very left-wing group fighting on behalf of struggling pensioners. They had their feet on the ground. Not surprisingly, some were Catholics and others had lapsed from Church membership. There was also a Jewish ex-Communist. They were pleased to have a left-wing cleric in their midst. They had known poverty at first hand and knew what it did to people.

I had a letter published in the *Glasgow Herald* about Carfin Grotto recalling that Edwin Muir in his *Scottish Journey* had described it as the only bright spot in darkest Lanarkshire. It had been built between the wars by unemployed miners. There was a proposal to erect a monument in the Grotto to the victims of the Irish Famine. The local MP Frank Roy thought this was sectarian. It was a typical effort to keep religion and politics separate. As a Catholic he should have known the origins of the shrine lay in the poverty of the people.

On another occasion I was asked to give a talk at Paisley Abbey about its monastic origins and to talk about its great drain, part of which had recently been uncovered. Medieval monasteries were built to similar plans. They had to make sure fresh water could get in and refuse drain away. It was said a blind Cistercian would know his way around any European monastery once he knew the water system. Medieval monks are seldom thought of as sanitary engineers. The Church is seen as encased instead in doctrine and ritual. Once upon a time it took part in initiatives that made a difference to people's lives.

In June 1999 I joined a bike ride from Edinburgh to the G8 meeting in Cologne as part of the Jubilee Campaign to cancel Third World debt, which had become a major campaigning issue. The meeting was next to the cathedral and Tony Blair came out to speak with us. In 2001 there was chaos during the G8 in Genoa as protests about Third World poverty became violent. After that these meetings to plan the economy of the world were held in inaccessible places so that the wealthy politicians couldn't be pestered by voices raised on behalf of the poor.

The G8 meeting for the year 2000 was to be held in Japan. To make sure no protesters could disrupt it the Japanese organised it in the far southern island of Okinawa. I knew some of the Italian Xaverians who were working in Japan so I joined them in Osaka for a month. It was possible to talk with some Japanese Justice and Peace groups who were aware of Japan's part in the global economy. I visited a Zen monastery in Nagasaki, where the second nuclear bomb had been dropped beside the Catholic cathedral. On the 55th anniversary of Hiroshima I was able to be present at a vast demonstration. Travelling in Japan it was very striking that in the midst of all the hi-tech certain ancient cultural practices had survived. In his book *The Lady and the Monk* Pico Iyer attributes this to a respect for tradition even amongst the young. Culture is something that is shared amongst the rich and the poor together.

I was also able to visit Cuba after a holiday with a niece who was working at the opposite end of the Caribbean, in Trinidad. It didn't feel like a Communist country. There were plenty of police around but they seemed intent on maintaining good behaviour on the streets. Business, at least for tourists, was conducted in American dollars. There was no sign of destitution. It seemed that despite the United States embargo on trade they had been able to introduce Western standards in health, education and welfare.

I biked with a group on the Camino, the pilgrimage to Santiago de Compostela. It was a wonderful experience of Spanish hospitality. The *refugios* (hostels) offered a bed at next to no cost. When one of us blew a tyre the owner of a bike shop fixed it for the promise of a prayer at Santiago. There were real pilgrims on the route who depended on the charity of others for food and drink. Encouraged to give something back, I became the Scottish representative on the board of the Confraternity of St James in London.

I was able to persuade my great friend, the former Moderator of the Church of Scotland, John Miller, to take time off at the Millennium. John was a hard-working minister in the Castlemilk housing scheme. I persuaded him that the so-called 'Millennium bug' would infect so many computers that nobody would be able to work during the first couple of weeks of January 2000. We drove to Land's End on New Year's Day 2000 and set off by bike, arriving at John O'Groats on 15 January. The roads, as we suspected, were mostly empty and the only snow we saw was at Drumochter Pass. John raised money for his daughter, who was working as a doctor in Zimbabwe. I had heard that Emmaus, a homelessness charity founded in France by the Abbé Pierre – who had been a hero of mine when I was a student in Rome – was opening in Glasgow. I raised £2,000 for it. It was to be my entry into work with the homeless.

25

Two Parishes

At the David Livingstone Centre in Blantyre there used to be a photograph of a priest hanging on one of the walls. It was Father Daniel Gallagher, to whom Livingstone had gone for the Latin lessons he needed to enter university. It is salutary to think that Gallagher, brought up in impoverished Ireland, had received a better education than what was available to Livingstone in nineteenth-century Scotland. When I found myself in St Simon's, the church which Gallagher had founded, I went back to the Centre. It had been refurbished and the photo had disappeared. I thought I might have hallucinated but the staff assured me the story was correct. Unfortunately, there had been no room for the priest's picture in the new set-up.

Livingstone used to walk into Glasgow to save money and I decided, in his memory, to retrace his footsteps. Glasgow Council had opened up the Clyde Walkway from Partick. Beyond the city boundary the track was overgrown. Gradually I was able to hack my way through the undergrowth around Newton to the pathway past Bothwell Castle to the Livingstone Centre. It then became possible to lead each year a pilgrimage alongside the river from Partick. This was recognised by the Centre in time for the bicentenary of Livingstone's birth in 2012. Pilgrimage is one way to open up people's hearts and minds to the physical basis of spirituality.

St Simon's was the third oldest Catholic church in the city, after the cathedral and St Mary's Calton. It is the oldest building in Partick still in its original use. Gallagher had enormous difficulty in getting anyone to rent him space for Catholic worship in Partick. An upstairs flat used as a school was referred to as 'Paddy's Castle'. For the first Mass all he could get was a former pest house. The roof leaked so badly that the umbrella that was used to shelter him became a parish heirloom. Despite this he was prominent in dissuading his congregation during sectarian troubles from joining the Fenian Movement. This might have been because his assistant priest came from the Orange part of Holland! The only trouble I had was a couple of break-ins. Vandals knew there was money in Catholic presbyteries.

The church Father Gallagher built, which he called St Peter's, eventually proved too small. Given what we know of the limited financial resources of Catholics at that time, it is astonishing that his successor, the legendary Dean McNair, acquired a whole acre in the middle of Partick to build first of all a school and secondly a large replacement church which took over the name of St Peter's in 1903. The old church became the Partick Bridge Street Hall before it was pressed back into service at weekends for Mass for the dock side of the main road. During the week it was used for billiards. The local housing was old tenements which served the poorer part of Partick. Very interestingly, in his memoirs Dr Harry Whitley, minister in Partick and later Moderator of the Church of Scotland, claimed to have lost half his congregation when he insisted that both sides of the main road – the poor and the better-off – should worship together in the same building.

The old church was reopened as a parish after World War Two. It was called St Simon's, the original name of the Apostle Peter. Later the Simon Community (named after Simon of Cyrene) ran a soup kitchen outside the church after Sunday Mass. We renovated the small hall which was used for storage and converted it into a café for use by the homeless. The idea was that there were so many cafés in the West End it would be good if there were one where the poor could be welcomed at no cost. Those who used it appreciated that it was not just another soup kitchen. At the beginning the Simon Community wanted to impose a range of health and safety restrictions but eventually the management was left to volunteers who had a more relaxed approach. The congregation met the expenses and a local businessman provided sandwiches with ROKPA, the Buddhist social wing, providing soup. Apart from the occasional drunk or mental health issue there was little trouble. The homeless even knew not to smoke because, they said, they noticed there were no ashtrays.

After the death of Pope John Paul II Historic Scotland made a grant of £200,000 to refurbish St Simon's since it served also as 'the Polish Chapel'. TV images had shown the building to be in poor condition. We had to match-fund. Fortunately there was £100,000 in the parish bank, leaving us to fundraise the other £100,000. We visited St Margaret's in Ayr, which had been beautifully restored by Father Pat Keegan, the priest who was in Lockerbie when the Pan Am jet was blown up. We decided to renew St Simon's in a similarly comprehensive way. The roof was reslated. The new Poles painted the inside with their customary good workmanship. We thought there might be a clash among the workers but the main difference was that the Scots went to Greggs while the Poles brought salads. Modern lighting was installed and an oak floor laid. The stained glass, which was amongst the earliest in Glasgow, was taken out and cleaned.

The congregation still represented the more dissident part of Catholicism but inevitably they were dubbed by others as the 'Wee Twees'. St Simon's resembled St Alphonsus not only because it attracted people from elsewhere, it was also due to celebrate its 150th anniversary. Not many priests are asked to manage two such occasions. We set about a three-year programme of renewal not only of the building but also of the congregation. We started the programme by having Mass on spare ground as near as possible to where we thought the first Mass had been said in the pest house. Archbishop Conti thought we were kidding. He hoped we would process to the place and then return to the church for Mass. A marquee protected him from the rain, which we were pleased to see since we had sold commemorative umbrellas for the occasion.

One of the parish council was a lecturer in accountancy. He believed that church-giving was a charism that needed to be taken more seriously. We abolished the passing of the plate. Catholics think this is giving their money away but in fact it is mostly needed to maintain the church buildings, in other words for themselves. They should pay that, like everything else, through the bank. When they were encouraged to do this they were embarrassed to say how little they put in the plate. So we actually got more. And they didn't even need to come to church! Thereafter we only passed the plate for special occasions to raise money for good causes. Legacies were still unusual in the Catholic Church, where wealth was only beginning to appear among the *nouveau riche*. A wealthy daily Mass attender in St Peter's died and left nothing to the church. A convert left St Simon's its first bequest. This was followed by another from a regular attender, who left instructions that there was to be no funeral as she had left her body to medical science.

In the refurbishment we had replaced the pews with chairs so that the building could have multiple uses. After all, pews had only been brought in at the Reformation so that the congregation could listen to lengthy expositions of the Bible from the minister. Fixed pews inhibit the natural movement of Catholic worship. In Rome the churches had few pews. San Egidio in Trastevere was able to serve a Christmas dinner to the poor in the open spaces of the church. With a quick shifting of chairs St Simon's became available for different purposes. One was a Seder meal during Holy Week. Another was an annual Burns Supper to thank all those who had volunteered for ministry during the year.

We opened the church during the day so that people could pop in to pray – or even just use the toilets. Mass was shifted to the more accessible time of 12.30 p.m. On Sundays music became important, with the parts of the Mass sung to various compositions. This was led by Sandra and Dermot Lamb with an old friend of mine from Broomhill days, Michael Ferguson, on the organ. The Poles used a projector for simultaneous translation. This gave us the idea of using their screen with PowerPoint. Not only did we save paper but the congregation sang much better with their heads raised to a screen rather than buried in a hymn book or missalette. We produced a quarterly newsletter called *Keynotes*. I achieved one of my ambitions by having the Easter Vigil start at dawn, so that from the dark we went into the sunrise rather than starting at dusk and ending up in the dark. One year the rising sun broke through into the church just as the Easter Eucharist began.

After my donation to the Emmaus Community for their Glasgow initiative, raised by my cycle from Land's End to John O'Groats, they invited me to join the committee. The founding board was mostly made up of members from St Mary's Episcopal and Hillhead Baptist churches. No sooner had I joined than the chairperson went off to England and I was appointed in his place. My experience on the board of Age Concern Scotland proved very useful. I also remembered the little book by the TUC president Walter Citrine on how to chair meetings.

I soon found out my donation was as nothing, since it was going to cost us more than a million to build. The money was not for the poor but for the architects and other professional services. We had difficulty finding a place. We looked at a run-down Catholic church nearby but Cardinal Winning was unwilling to close a church. The parish priest of Our Lady of the Assumption, Ruchill, Father John Lyons, did us a great turn by giving us a second-hand goods shop which he had. Under the able leadership of Celia MacIntosh this proved a goldmine for Emmaus.

Our search for a site ended when the Grove church in Hamiltonhill, which wanted to move to the main road in Possilpark, nominated us as preferred buyers of their property. Emmaus UK, whose president was Terry Waite, loaned us the asking price of £100,000. By the time Terry came up to open it for 24 companions, as Emmaus residents are called, we had spent £2.1 million. This came one quarter from European finance, one quarter from the Scottish government and one quarter from Glasgow City Council. The remaining half million we had to raise ourselves and we were particularly helped by (Lord) Willie Haughey. The first companions arrived in January 2006, not long after the death at 94 of Abbé Pierre.

I was asked to take a turn on the board of Emmaus UK but this turned out to be a waste of time. The charity, like others, was heading in the direction of paying staff salaries equivalent to the public rather than the voluntary sector. The first community, Cambridge, resisted this and left the UK organisation. What was more useful to me was meeting with the other chairs of communities, because it was with the chairs that the buck stopped. At one point I had to raise an emergency loan of £10,000 from our own board.

I went to a meeting of the Christian Socialist Movement, which some in England wanted to see stronger in Scotland. I became the treasurer and was surprised to be told that we were expected to affiliate to the Labour Party. I had to explain that in Scotland there was another party Christian socialists might join, namely the Scottish National Party. This provoked incomprehension. Many years previously some of us in Justice and Peace had tried to join the Labour Party as a group but the old hands had thought we were a nuisance. The Labour Party in London had little idea of the changes that were taking place in Scotland. They were intent on capturing the middle ground. They were no longer the voice of the poor. I was invited to speak to the Scottish Parliament at Holyrood and was warmly greeted as her 'favourite priest' by the assisted-dying campaigner and MSP Margo MacDonald of the SNP.

A different kind of poverty was present in the West End among older people. They belonged to that generation which for the first time had more money from their pensions than they had been able to earn when they were working. Often their family had moved away or were busy working. Essentially they were 'shut in'. Loneliness is bad for health. It was sad to see some who had been eminent figures in the university reduced to having to shop alone. We started up an Ascent Group. This was inspired by the French movement, *La Vie Ascendant*, to face the challenges of spirituality in older life.

Glasgow City Council arranged a visit from an American Jesuit, Father Greg Boyle, who had founded Homeboys Industry in Los Angeles for gang members. All the great and the good were there, none of whom, significantly, I recognised from street work. Many would have been lapsed Catholics who would have had no clue how to respond to a priest advocating the rights of the poor. Nor were any of them in a position to offer employment to gang members. They would have seen no virtue in poverty. The scale of poverty was greater in the USA but there was also a greater diversity of response. Some of the rich there felt the need to enable others to pull themselves up. In Scotland the newly well-off did not feel any call to share their new wealth with the poor.

26

Homeless Jesus

What if I had stayed on in the West End of the city and hadn't got any experience of life in the East End? Poverty might have remained an interest, possibly at an academic level. Moving to the deprived Bridgeton, against my own feelings at the time, made it all very real. I came into contact and made friends with many who were working at the coalface. It became possible to contemplate moving to Bangladesh, considered at the time to be one of the most poverty-stricken places on Earth.

Justin Martyr, the defender of the Christians against their Roman persecutors, said that apart from reading the Scriptures in their assemblies they also remembered those who were absent from them, especially widows and orphans. This has all but disappeared from the remembrance of Jesus in today's Communion service. Congregations may complain about the number of collections but most are for maintenance, not for mission; they are for the churches themselves, not for outreach. There may be little sense that the congregation is part of a greater church. Mention might be made of those who cannot attend, like the sick and the old, but it is purely notional. The more vulnerable are not only shut in but shut out.

Embracing poverty voluntarily is an imitation of Jesus. That is what Christians are supposed to be called to. It is the best way to know oneself, stripped of as much distraction as possible, giving us hope that we can find out the truth about ourselves and our place in the world. St Paul urged the better-off among his converts to take up a collection for those worse off than themselves. He was also anxious to let his listeners know that he worked to provide for himself (as a tent maker).

The influence of Celtic monasticism on the Church has been significant with respect to poverty. Ireland as an island was able to keep some of the stricter ideals inherited from the original eastern spirituality. Irish monks generally were not ordained as priests. Their charism therefore was not obedience to a bishop: it was poverty. Lay people could live a simple lifestyle in harmony with the whole of creation. Now the question is: can an individual today become 'a monk in the world'. The first monks had wanted to be away from it all and built their monasteries in inaccessible places like Skellig Michael in the Atlantic off the west coast of Ireland. The great Benedictine monasteries of the Middle Ages combined work and prayer – *laborare est orare* (to work is to pray). They revolutionised agriculture, and market towns sprang up beside them. After the Reformation monastic renewal emphasis was on the solemn celebration of a robust liturgical practice that was faithful to the past but allowed also contemporary influences. All three of these aspects speak to us today. We are not to listen to the dead voices of the living exhorting us to mindless repetition. It is the living voices of the dead that encourage us to imitate them.

At one time churches were part of the local market. They were the spaces where people gathered. Catholics now focus on the reservation of the sacrament. Churches have become places for spiritual exercises only. Religion has made space for the soul at the expense of the body. This has suited the better-off. The historian Eric Hobsbawm recorded that when Anglicans during the Industrial Revolution began fundraising to build churches in poorer areas, a workman said he would give a penny to hang a bishop but not to build a church; disillusionment with the Church was so complete that people did not want it. In every town or village can be seen spires that are meant to raise our minds to heaven. They might have done that at one time but now they are being closed and turned into flats, restaurants or art venues because people's hopes today are horizontal rather than vertical. Most large churches are redundant unless they can convert their space to social use.

The needs of societies which contain both rich and poor are not easily met. The cry for revolution has been heard down the ages. There is a Gospel reservation about violence to achieve justice. Revolutions usually manage to devour their own. We need organic intellectuals after the manner of Gramsci, the Italian Marxist. In prison, crippled by a spine disease, he wrote of the need for pessimism of the intellect and optimism of the will. If we think of what needs to be done we can easily despair. For Christians optimism is the virtue of hope which overcomes all odds.

For Pope Francis the imitation of the poverty of Jesus is more important than the habit of clerical obedience. He proposed that the model of the Church should be a field hospital where those who are most in need can get help. Francis of Assisi lived at the beginning of banking and realised he didn't want anything to do with a system that would help the rich to consolidate their wealth. The banks today are still proving him right.

In 2013, on the Feast of St Francis, the poor man of Assisi, I retired from St Simon's in a campervan. Someone asked what I did with all my books. I bought an iPad which had a Kindle app. But in our regulated society it is not easy to simplify one's life. I joined the Thousand Huts movement, which seeks legal reforms in land use that make it easier to have access to a cabin, shed, hut. I had known from my Justice and Peace days a landowner who was sympathetic to land reform and who had several huts on his estate. I was able to negotiate the use of one of those and relocate it at the edge of a wood some distance from the road. On the 50th anniversary of my ordination I received the keys. We have to advocate a political change that will allow older people to reduce themselves to a simpler – and poorer – way of life.

Some of the figures relating to land use are revealing. At a time when good farm land was priced at about £2,900 per acre, it would be valued at £267,000 if it was sold for building houses. If there was planning permission, it would be worth £613,000. No wonder we see new-builds where food used to be grown. A lawyer associated with Justice and Peace said that in Europe Scotland came closest to the large landholdings that in South America are called *latifundia*. However, much land in Scotland is not arable. Landowners have to struggle with the variables of capital and technology. It has occurred to some that there is commercial value in making land available for hutting so that, as in other northern European countries, people can escape from the demands of urban living.

Alan Bennett's story of *The Lady in the Van* is a sobering one. He let someone living on the street park in his driveway. How many of us would do that? Would we find a place in our home for a refugee? St Martin-in-the-Fields in the centre of London allows the homeless to sleep in the pews overnight. Those who still go to church for worship complain about the lack of ministers and priests to lead the service. Rather than vicars we need leaders who are able to maintain a simple lifestyle in the midst of consumerism. The Anglican theologian, Oliver Davies, advocates compassion as the way forward. On the occasion of Abbé Pierre's centenary in 2012 I had an article published about 'the uprising of kindness' he experienced when he set up the first Emmaus Community during a severe winter in Paris.

The landowner R.B. Cunninghame Graham, the first socialist MP in Scotland and the founder of the Scottish National Party, lived much of his life overseas in a hard way. When he returned to Scotland he said: 'All that is left to reasonable men is to pay the bootmakers' and tailors' bills with regularity, give alms to the deserving and the undeserving poor, and then live humbly under the sun, taking example from the other animals.' It reminds me of the story of the wealthy man who died suddenly. A friend asked: 'How much did he leave?' Came the answer: 'He left it all.' Another story is of a rich man visiting a hermit and asking him where his furniture was. The hermit said: 'I don't see you with any.' The rich man replied that he was only a visitor. 'So am I,' said the hermit. We should be detached from our possessions.

After I retired there came a request out of the blue from a Canadian sculptor: Timothy P. Schmalz had made a sculpture of a figure lying on a park bench covered with a blanket and only the feet sticking out. The feet were pierced. He called it *Homeless Jesus*. He offered it to the cathedral in his home town of Toronto. But they declined, saying Jesus had risen and was no longer homeless. He had a nice place in the tabernacle in the church. The Jesuits took it and placed it in downtown Regis College. Copies have since been erected in various cities throughout the world. Schmalz asked if one could be set up in Glasgow. This required, reasonably enough, a complex planning procedure. There was some apprehension that it would become a political issue. Such fears proved unfounded and permission was granted to place the sculpture, with the support of the minister and congregation, behind St George's Tron in the city centre. A young fellow I knew who could sing and became one of the cantors in St Alphonsus told me he had once been reduced through addiction to sleeping on a park bench. He simply ignored those who abused him. What he remembered was those who gave him a friendly look or a compassionate smile. It was hoped that the *Homeless Jesus* icon would encourage a similar response to beggars.

With respect to poverty issues I came to two conclusions. The first is local and refers to the provision of health care, which the poor need most. The poor used to be thin and the rich fat. Now the rich are slim and the poor obese. The National Health Service has become the National Disease Service. Disease affects the old more than the young. The question arises about how to manage the present needs of the aged and infirm. My solution, as a socialist, is to make the health service free to those under 21. After that people would only remain under the NHS if they had a chronic condition resulting from childhood disease. From 21 everyone should be required to insure themselves, as Beveridge himself had intended. Nobody would be left to die in the street – but neither would hospital staff be taken for granted by those who have not taken reasonable care of themselves.

The other conclusion is about overseas aid. No country should qualify for this unless, like the donor countries, they are having elections every four or five years. Otherwise aid becomes trade which helps the host country and keeps the poorest countries still within the Western cash nexus. Even worse, it could be a trade in arms which fuels the constant local warfare. This mostly affects Africa. It is the home of most of the minerals which the developed world wants, yet it is becoming more impoverished by the day. After the 9/11 attack in New York it occurred to me for the first time that I would not live to see violence in the world eliminated. The vision of a new 'Islamic State' came from the oldest of religious beliefs – that of an afterlife.

I visited a niece teaching in Qatar in order to see the conditions Bangladeshi workers were living in while they built the stadiums for the World Cup. Not surprisingly, the workers preferred to send their comparatively high wages back to Bangladesh rather than spend them improving the conditions they would only be living in for a limited period of time.

In the 2010 film *The Way* Martin Sheen embarks on the

pilgrimage to Santiago de Compostela because his son, according to the story, died in a storm on the way. When we did the Camino in 1998 it was still fairly primitive. It has now become enormously popular. There is a bit of a debate about who is entitled to call themselves a pilgrim. Do you have to have a religious intention? This is interpreted fairly widely at the cathedral in Santiago, where they stamp the passport of the places you have passed through. The film finds room for everybody, whether they are doing the walk religiously or not. The most common denominator is that those on the way have mostly stripped themselves down to the essentials. They are willing to depend on the hospitality provided. One Franciscan priest walked it in his habit without money and lacked for nothing over the six weeks. There is plenty of food and shelter for everybody in the world. We need to be converted by our pilgrimage through life to share what we have with others. This is the real meaning of poverty.

We are all 'Jock Tampson's bairns'. In a world divided between the haves and the have-nots there is evidence that equality makes for a better community. If we took from our garage or from under the bed what we haven't used in the last year and gave it away, somebody else would enjoy it. With respect to the Third World the choice is even more stark. The coltan we need for our mobile phones comes from the east of the Democratic Republic of the Congo, which has consequently become a bloodbath of competing factions. We are bargaining with the lives of the poor. There is a whole range of commodities for which we should be willing to pay a little more so that mothers who are at present too poor to do so can feed their own children. We are called to heal the broken-hearted.

Part 3
Celibacy

27

World without Sex

There was sex in 1940 – obviously! It just wasn't talked about. Nor was it all repressed, as Freud had alleged. The 1948 American Kinsey study on sexual behaviour was repeated the following year in the UK by Mass Observation. The findings were never published. 'Little Kinsey' said that there was premarital sex, cohabitation and homosexuality despite the taboos that prevented them from being the subjects of conversation. World War Two had an effect. During the war sex had to be grabbed where it could be found, with a certain amount of urgency. With men away from home so much it was more difficult to arrange a marriage ceremony. Unmentioned was the fact that the military was entirely masculine. Male bonding was a necessity, as men were thrust into close quarters with each other whether in the front line or in back room bunkers. At the same time, the report revealed that over one third of respondents thought it was possible to live without sex.

The movies are an indicator of the attitudes of the time. The 1940s were the peak of the cinema-going age. Hollywood wanted to sell sex but was restricted by the Hays Code and the Catholic League of Decency. It was joked that it was run by Jews for Protestants with Catholic morality. Most romantic films were of the Mills and Boon variety of fictional love, even if there were double entendres. There were well-founded rumours that leading actresses often had complicated personal lives. They had multiple sexual relationships and were introduced to narcotics. Yet they were presented with virginal purity. There were 'bodice rippers' with full bosoms and suggestive situations. The audiences packed out the cinemas, loving the medium and getting the message. 'Going to the pictures' was particularly popular in Scotland. Glasgow had the most cinemas per head of population in the UK. It was a place for couples to cuddle.

At the time of the Second World War life was still physically demanding. Most men did work that required bodily labour. At weekends they crowded into football matches and drank together in pubs. Women cooked and cleaned with equipment that required a lot of effort. They were regularly photographed wearing aprons and a scarf containing their curls. The main supply of heat was a coal fire, which was dirty and needed daily maintenance. It supplied a bath on a weekly basis, 'whether needed or not' as Good Queen Bess said of her annual wash. Children were expected to get dirty when they were out playing. Kettles were boiled for the washing of clothes which were then run through a mangle before being hung outside to dry.

The physicality appeared not to include sex. If not out of mind, it was out of sight. Births were surrounded with talk of storks delivering babies. Family life was supposed to mean domestic bliss. 'Early to bed, early to rise' was the motto. What people did in between was their business. There was no central heating. After the coal fire went out, bed was the warmest place to be. There was no television to keep people up.

In 1940 child abuse meant physical neglect, not sexual interference. 'Green ladies' (health visitors) visited new mothers to make sure everything was all right with a new child. They were highly visible with their leather bags (which children thought contained the new babies). Any suspicion that all was not well could mean a visit from the 'Cruelty Woman', the forerunner of social-work departments. Children could get knocked about in their own home. A kick in the backside could be administered by neighbours and even passers-by. Policemen were intimidating figures, not to say bogeymen called upon to frighten. Physical punishment was the rule both in borstals and in the poshest schools. There was no open hint of anything that might resemble sex abuse. This is not to say it didn't exist. It just wasn't in the public forum. Incest was known to occur but was thought to be without lasting effects.

Some people didn't get married – for all sorts of reasons. Men tended to marry later and some were unsuccessful in finding a partner. Women were beginning to get careers for themselves. War, with men away fighting, had thrust women into public work. Some of these jobs, like primary teaching, excluded marriage. In central and local government women had to resign on getting married. Many eldest daughters remained unmarried in order to look after their parents. Maiden aunts were a familiar figure to children. 'Bohemian' types may have indulged in sexual shenanigans but were not imitated. For most, casual sex was not an option: with the lack of reliable contraception the unmarried mother (and her child) were looked down upon.

All authorities tended to be strict, not to say prudish. Pleasure was to be carefully measured. The churches were strict on sexual morality. Many families were large, not only Catholic ones. Married and unmarried alike had to follow the same rules. Girls especially were expected to be chaste before marriage and faithful after it. Those who didn't marry were expected to manage somehow. There was no stigma attached to being single. There were bachelors (men) and spinster ladies. The word celibacy, as a virtuous state in itself, was not used.

28

Boys Will Be Boys

Boys and girls mixed first in families and then in school. In Penilee the Catholics had at first two classrooms in the non-denominational but de facto 'Protestant' school. At playtime we were afforded one quarter of the yard. Boys being boys there was occasional stone-throwing. However, I was invited to go round all the classrooms to show the artwork my father had provided for Christmas. He had to go to work on Christmas Day, after having been to Midnight Mass. The Scottish winter holiday was New Year – Hogmanay and Ne'erday. The 'first foot' into the house after midnight on 1 January – always by a man – was taken seriously. Neighbours were invited into each other's houses to share a drink with shortbread. By tradition, for Hogmanay, wives bought the alcohol out of the weekly shopping budget. There was a joke about a woman buying the booze and popping a loaf on top. Her man asked: 'What's all the food for?'

Boys and girls had the same classrooms but the boys' desks were on one side of the room and the girls' on the other. There were certain activities for girls only – sewing and knitting – while the boys did woodwork. There were different toys – dolls for girls, cars for boys. Girls played netball and rounders, boys football and cricket. Boys had marbles (we had 'bools', ball bearings taken from the Rolls-Royce factory), girls had skipping ropes. Boys joined the Cubs and Scouts, girls the Brownies and the Guides. Boys were taken to football games with their fathers. Girls helped their mothers or played at 'shops'. It was left to boys and girls to work out among themselves the curiosities of their differences, of which they became increasingly aware. Not all games were completely innocent. Most families seemed to have both sons and daughters, although large families were already unusual. One boy on the other side of the street was an only child, which was rare.

Boys and girls were brought up as equal but separate. Of the small group jockeying for position at the top of our primary class there were as many girls as boys. It made for confidence among both. In fact the girls might have been more ambitious. In our class several of them became teachers, while most of the boys took up apprenticeships alongside their fathers and uncles. Already girls were thinking not just of getting married but of getting jobs. There were many local opportunities. It was no longer presumed that a woman's place was in the home. Women could have lives of their own. They were more active than men in the local area. My mother had five sisters. They all met every other Sunday in the family home to play whist, a card game. A spinster aunt took responsibility for keeping the nieces and nephews in order. When tea was being served the aunts would hitch their skirts and jostle for a place along the kitchen range to heat their bottoms. The children, naturally, were intrigued by this unusual display of underwear.

What was it like to live in a family with an older sister and a younger brother? An older girl would be trusted more easily by parents to look after the house if they were out. Boys were inclined to fight, for instance over the D.C. Thomson comics which were a staple conversation diet – *Wizard* and *Adventure* on a Tuesday, *Rover* and *Hotspur* on a Thursday. Not every family bought them all. They were shared among classmates. The belt or 'strap' wasn't used much in St George's School. My mother protested vigorously when my sister was 'strapped' by a male teacher. Corporal punishment was generally thought to promote 'manliness'. Pupils were controlled by the 'Lochgelly', named after the place where the tawse was made. Teachers who made generous use of it strongly defended themselves against charges of sadism, although some did take more pleasure in it than others. In cases that reached the courts, teachers were exonerated. Getting 'six of the best' (of the belt) was the stuff of which certain boys were made into school heroes.

Besides school the other influence was the Catholic parish. In 1948, with post-war restrictions on building materials in place, the priests constructed a large Nissen hut whose corrugated iron roof constantly leaked. This chapel doubled as a hall and was the focus of religious and social activities for Catholics. When I was old enough I applied to become an altar boy. I was keen to see what the priest actually did on the altar. Many of his actions were difficult to discern from the body of the church, shrouded as he was in large vestments and incense smoke. I was attracted by the sense of mystery without having any idea of its sacramental import. If anything, being an altar boy lessened the mystery. Much mischief was associated with altar boys. One Midnight Mass lacked some solemn sounds because one boy held on to the gong while I kept hold of the striker. I couldn't say serving at the altar was a particularly religious experience. Focus was on learning the Latin responses by heart, without understanding. Other writers recall play-acting the part of the priest, but we were too mischievous for that.

Being an altar boy was not the only activity girls were excluded from. They weren't considered for the school football team either. It didn't strike us as odd that the priests were all men. So were bus drivers. In the church it was taken for granted that the men would look after the grounds and the women would do the cleaning. This was what happened in the home. It seemed the natural state of affairs. On the other hand, most primary teachers were women. The writer Donny O'Rourke has a wonderful poem about his first schoolteacher – Miss Hughes, 'dream colleen and crabbit queen of primary one'. She was 'a stickler for proper English and Catholic self-improvement'. He owed to her 'every word I've ever read or written'.

Did keeping boys and girls apart like this promote or hinder their development? They shared the same toilets at home – why did the facilities have to be separated elsewhere? At the prepubertal stage there was no great emphasis on the differences between the sexes or questions of mutual respect. There was a certain competitiveness between boys and girls. It would be later before this resulted in the stereotypical behaviour that would be described as sexism.

29

Seminary

When people ask, with some degree of incredulity, 'if you went away at twelve years old to study for the priesthood, how could you have any idea of what it might entail?' The answer is, of course, one had no idea. The word 'seminary' comes from the Latin *semen*, meaning seed. It is a place where the seed of a calling is to be nurtured. It is a place where wild seeds should not be sown. Some boys who went to Blairs left quite quickly, finding the regime too strict. Others were told to leave or not return, having been judged by the staff as unsuitable. This was usually not for any breaking of rules but for inability at studies.

There was no presumption that because you were at Blairs you would succeed in becoming a priest. Of the 54 boys who joined with me only 21 went on to study for the priesthood at a senior level. Many left before ordination, deciding they did not have 'a vocation'. Eventually only 11 became priests. Far from there being any pressure to stay there was a regular winnowing out of those who appeared unsure about what they were supposed to be preparing for. The truth is we were probably fairly average boys from church-going families who might have felt inspired by the priests they had known to have a shot at becoming one themselves. I had an older cousin who was a Marist Brother teaching in Africa. He visited occasionally and was held in much respect.

The purpose of boarding schools generally was first of all to turn boys into men and, secondly, to separate, as it has been put, the men from the goats. Boarding schools have been compared to closed institutions, like prisons and asylums. It would be naive to think that everyone would recover from that type of education. The outbreak of the First World War was blamed by some on men who were removed from their families at an early age and given a militaristic schooling. The effect of this kind of 'muscular

Christianity' on some who became priests seems obvious, first of all, in their interest in sport. It also became clear that some thought of themselves as of a 'higher caste' and bullied those over whom they claimed authority.

In the context of residential schooling there arises the question of sexual abuse by older boys or members of staff. There must have been awareness in Blairs of the potential risk since the rules were observed with extreme severity. We slept in dormitories but in separate cubicles, with only a curtain as a partition making interference very difficult. Entering another's cubicle or even visiting the dormitory by day was met with instant expulsion. You were not allowed to mix with a different year group. Even within your own age group what were known as 'particular friendships' were noted and discouraged. There was a rule against 'laying on of hands', which was not to prevent fighting but to nip in the bud any incipient intimacy. From after supper until breakfast a 'Grand Silence' was strictly observed.

The French writer Ernest Renan, who attended St Sulpice Seminary in Paris in the 1830s, commented then on these features of seminary life. In my time both the rector and the Master of Discipline had attended St Sulpice. It remained, in the twentieth century, notorious for the severity of its regime. Some of the Blairs staff appeared to be ascetic intellectuals. We admired more the ones who played football and cricket. With regard to religious practice it would be fair to say that the emphasis was on saying prayers rather than learning how to pray.

The only sexual experience I remember was during the holidays when I was touched on a bus by an older boy from Blairs. The holidays gave him an opportunity he didn't have in term time. I got off at the next stop. The writer Teresa Breslin said she went to a convent school and wasn't abused: 'But, hey, you can't have everything,' she added. There was no corporal punishment in Blairs. For its time this was progressive. Certainly some older boys hit younger boys when they could get away with it. When I arrived there were College customs that allowed older boys to administer a kick in the pants to younger boys who had still to learn certain traditions.

Most boys had sisters and had played with girls. 'Catholic guilt' wasn't much in evidence. A small number of boys in Blairs were afflicted by scruples. This was no mere scrupulosity for it was accompanied by nervous tics. This might be put down to competitiveness around religious devotions. I can remember being tempted to do the Stations of the Cross with greater fervour than others. When we went at 18 to senior seminary we were joined by boys who had attended day schools. There wasn't much difference with respect to sexual experiences in those days irrespective of what school you went to. Everyone was relatively 'pure'.

Dancing was where boys and girls first begin to interact and in those days that didn't start until after secondary school. There were still many schools that were single sex, including all boarding schools. Where boys and girls attended the same school probably the most they would get up to together would be mischief. There are plenty of autobiographies of those who were at school in the 1950s. Hardly any of them, until recently, mention sex. Some thought the physical discipline was a good thing. Others rebelled against the general restrictions that were imposed. Some of these limitations were due to post-war austerity. TV only became popular after the coronation of the new queen in 1953. Serious newspapers still had adverts on the front page. The boldest boys would sneak into health shops, where they could get pictures of naked women which could then be surreptitiously passed around. The first person I thought I might be in love with was Debbie Reynolds, star of *The Tender Trap* (1955).

'Dirty magazines' was the nearest boys got to sex education. These were not available in Blairs. There was weekly confession, where an aversion to 'touching yourself' was instilled. We were given the lives of the saints. These were the people we should aim to imitate. None of them were married. It didn't occur to us that this might not be normal. Not being married meant that you could have a more direct communion with God. St John Vianney, the Curé d'Ars, was proposed as an example for us. He was the patron saint of confession. He said that 'even if there were no after-life I would have done it all for the love of God'. In the Holy Week of my final year I thought Blairs had had the necessary spiritual effect for me to continue my studies at a senior level. I wrote in a notebook: 'I am so very happy. I do long for the priesthood. Yet what an unworthy instrument.' When I read this now as a priest embarrassment comes to mind.

The writer John Cornwell attended a junior seminary, Cotton College near Birmingham, at this time. He detailed his experience in *A Seminary Boy*, which included deviant and abusive priests. His recollections are quite different from mine. He came from a difficult background where poverty and mental illness were present. The impression is given of trying to compensate for these by an exaggerated religious enthusiasm. He reports going to the chapel in the middle of the night, which in Blairs would have been impossible. He also became obsessed by his sexual development. I don't remember adolescent angst as a major factor. I remember we wanted to be outdoors as much as possible in the extensive grounds. This may itself have been a form of sublimated sex. Sex itself was something confined to marriage. Nobody mentioned celibacy. The word was purity.

30

Invention of Sex

I took my promise of celibacy in 1963. That was the *annus mirabilis* of the poet Philip Larkin, who declared it was the year when sexual intercourse began – in the time, he said, between the legal trial over the publication of *Lady Chatterley's Lover* and the Beatles' first LP. In 'This Be The Verse' Larkin wrote: 'Man hands on misery to man. / It deepens like a coastal shelf. / Get out as early as you can, / And don't have any kids yourself.' It was the beginning of the 'permissive society' which meant particularly sexual liberalisation. People could begin to talk openly about sexual matters. Whatever went on before 1963, it was from about then that public taboos about sex gradually began to be overcome. It then became part of the mass media agenda. The press, cinema and then TV constantly pushed the boundaries. In 1964 the Golden Globe Best Film award went to Otto Preminger's *The Cardinal*. Religion with sex was big business. *The Nun's Story* (1959) starring the quasi-divine Audrey Hepburn was considered 'controversial' by the Church because at the end she left the convent or 'jumped over the wall' as it was put at the time.

You only have to look at the buttoned-up denizens of photographs before 1963 to realise that sex had not been a public activity. The decade turned into the Swinging Sixties. Wartime austerity for many was gradually forgotten. Not only buttons were loosened but also tongues. Skirts got shorter and bosoms were accentuated. People began to visit the Continent, where the locals held hands and kissed each other in public. Younger people in general began to smoke and drink, not unlike but more than their parents did. Some experimented with illegal drugs and with sex. Previously you had to get married to have sex, but the availability of the contraceptive pill (from 1961 it was possible to get it on the NHS) meant unintended pregnancy was less of a risk. Now marriage began to be talked about as bourgeois and repressive. What had been an essential social institution became more of a personal choice. Divorce rates increased steadily.

At this time there was still National Service, which was exclusively male. How influential was it upon those who were called up? Many complained that much of it was just standing about. Others learned a trade or saw parts of the world they wouldn't otherwise have seen. Some experienced actual combat, defending the Suez Canal or the last remains of the British Empire. It was not until 1957 that it was announced it would end and the last conscripts left only in 1963. Until that time there was still a strict demarcation in the activities of young men and young women.

What was it like to spend those years in an all-male environment with the prospect at the end of it of making a promise not to marry? It was accepted as the condition of becoming a priest. Pertinent questions may be raised about my years between the ages of 18 and 24, when most of my contemporaries were cultivating girlfriends with hopes of marriage and children. There was no question but that priests were unmarried. Therefore it didn't make any sense for those in a seminary to have a girlfriend. During the holidays one met girls. One of the criteria for staying or leaving would be whether one was more interested in girls than in getting ordained. It didn't occur to us at the time a reason for not being interested in girls might be homosexuality.

In an American book published in 1978 about the 100 most influential persons in history they are all men – with the single exception of Queen Elizabeth I of England scraping in at number 95. What is equally intriguing is the number who never married. Among those who did marry some had no children. There are two possible interpretations of this. One is that they were so intent on what they became famous for that they had no time for relationships. The other interpretation is that despite relationships they kept an inclination to individuality that facilitated their pursuit of military prowess or scientific endeavour. In either case it is possible that they also had homosexual inclinations. Men tend to marry at an older age than women, being able to procreate at any age. Bachelorhood for them has always been a more socially accepted status than spinsterhood for women. It was therefore easier for men not to marry at all. Kant and Wittgenstein, for example, never had intimate relationships, 'an exaggeration of traits which can be found in all of us', wrote the psychiatrist Anthony Storr.

If there was any sense of privilege among those destined for the Eternal City it had been immediately deflated in Blairs by the Master of Discipline, Father Danny Boyle, who had studied in France. 'The College in Rome is just a doss house,' he told us. This turned out to be partly true. All our studies took place in the Jesuit-run Gregorian University. Every morning before 8 a.m. we left the College near the Piazza Barberini, went down the Via Rasella (scene of a famous attack by Italian partisans on the German Army in World War Two) and turned at the Trevi Fountain into 'the Greg'. The lectures usually concluded in time for us to return to the College for lunch after which we had a short siesta. There was an hour's walk in the afternoon before study and recreation in the evening. The walk was to introduce us to the wonders of imperial, papal and modern Rome. Our day was therefore not only quite tightly organised but might reasonably described as 'modified monasticism'.

A visiting preacher, a Jesuit, told us: *serva ordinem et ordo te servabit* (make use of order and order will be useful to you). Even when making a cup of tea we should plan the procedure so that we didn't waste any effort. This was quite insightful, given the laissez-faire environment in which we lived. We struggled with the half-hour set aside for early morning meditation. A little mortification, it was assumed, would provide enough self-control. Philosophical stoicism was probably thought more important than a theology of the Cross on Calvary. An article in the Scottish Catholic historical magazine, the *Innes Review*, on seminaries concluded that Scottish seminarians were 'remarkably unremarkable'.

The rector of the Scots College, Monsignor William Clapperton, came from the Catholic enclave of the Enzie of Banff in Moray. He had been in Rome from the time when he had been a student himself, joining the staff immediately after ordination, and had become part of the Roman establishment. He had an air of having seen it all. He was fazed neither by know-nothing bishops nor know-it-all students. If you wanted to study hard, well and good. If you didn't, it was up to your bishop to find out. Once on a retreat in the Vatican he was translating from Italian for an American priest. The American congratulated him on his English and asked where he had learned it. 'Fochabers' was Clapperton's lugubrious reply. The Scots College wasn't as carefree as the College of the Beda, which was for mature students. It was said there that the only rules were not to light a cigarette from the sanctuary lamp or to have a woman in your room after 10 p.m.

Sport undoubtedly provided a degree of sublimation of sex. For most of the students playing football was very important. There were weekly matches amongst ourselves and games to be played against the other colleges. No fewer than five of our class immediately made the College football team during our first year. When we beat the English College 3–0 after years of defeat the rector, Monsignor Clapperton, not a sportsman at all, couldn't conceal his delight and ordered extra wine for supper. Keeping fit was thought to be good. In summer we had our own swimming pool and tennis courts at the villa near Marino in the Alban Hills.

The Scots College had a long tradition of putting on Gilbert and Sullivan operettas at Christmas. Half the cast, of course, is female. There was never any question but that a dozen or more students would be dressed as women during the three nights of production. That this was done fairly mindlessly by the Scots might be illustrated by the fact that it was not allowed in the North American College, which managed to produce *My Fair Laddie* without any female characters. Americans would have been more socially aware. We were helped by the fact that during the shows wine was provided in abundance from our own vineyard. There was a fairly raucous atmosphere in our little theatre.

One of the few times sex was mentioned was when a student preparing for the ordination ceremony told the rector that he had been advised he should be free of impure thoughts for at least six months before it. Clapperton replied that he hadn't been free of impure thoughts for six months either before or after taking his promise of celibacy. His successor, Phil Flanagan, was a much more inhibited Celt. He objected to nudity in the changing room at the pool. He didn't prevent students acting as women in Gilbert and Sullivan but he stopped Scottish country dancing as part of its preparation. The students who 'gave up' in Rome and who went back to Scotland mostly went on to secular studies in a university. None left in order to get married although they might have decided the single life was not for them. In those days men who had the chance of tertiary education usually only got married after they had secured a good job.

It is therefore not really surprising that sex was not a major issue even for those who were about to forswear it for the rest of their lives. A promise not to marry came as part of an initiation process. 'Minor orders' had responsibilities that were merely ritual, such as being a Reader at Mass. Being ordained as a sub-deacon was regarded as 'major' because it was when the promise of celibacy was made. It was a step not easily got back from. The procedure in Rome was relatively cavalier since there were hundreds of students from all the different colleges going through the process. The rector of each college had to make the request of the Roman authorities. The decision was his, taken no doubt in consultation with other members of staff. In the Scots College it seemed to work on the basis of *nihil obstat* (no objection) that is, if there was nothing objectionable in a student's general conduct he was allowed to proceed.

For each of the stages towards ordination we had to sit an exam at the Roman vicariate. The fat monsignor in charge was completely cynical. His job was to collect the fees for the ordination ceremonies. We had to mug up answers to questions such as could you smoke a cigarette while reciting the breviary? The correct answer, we were warned, was you couldn't start praying while you were smoking. But if while you were praying you needed a fag that was OK! 'The training was designed to develop a rugged individualism capable of withstanding the pressures of living alone, needing little companionship except that of God' (Martin Tierney, *No Second Chance: Reflections of a Dublin Priest*).

Our sub-diaconate service, when we made the promise of celibacy, was notable for its length because so many others from all over the world were being ordained to various orders at the same service. We had no relatives or friends present. Instead we were wakened early to get to the church on time. Since we knew the service would be long we went into a bar for a strong coffee before it. Already there at 6 a.m. was a pimp checking his girls after their night's work. He asked us what we, dressed in our purple cassocks, were doing up so early. When we explained we were on our way to make a promise of lifelong celibacy he expressed his admiration and wished us well. We didn't have time to reflect on his different choice!

Celibacy is not virginity. You don't have to be innocent to be a priest. Technically, celibacy means the condition of not being married, although it is commonly understood to be a vow not to indulge in sexual activity. In ancient times most priests probably were married. They married earlier and were ordained later. So it was possible for a man to have had a family and later take a promise of celibacy. From earliest times it was bishops who were not married. They then insisted on non-marriage for all clergy. It is generally agreed that the need for celibacy in the Catholic Church comes not from the Gospel but from the traditional way the Church is organised. It would be true to say that I made a promise not to get married without knowing much about sex. I'm sure others at the time got married not knowing any more. Newly ordained priests probably fitted more the category of bachelors than anything else. This was the kind of lifestyle they thought they were pledging themselves to.

There was no discussion about the consequences of celibacy. This was not only that the celibate couldn't attempt to get married, it was the giving-up of family life. There would be no having to get up in the middle of the night for a crying baby. Men who were looking to get married probably didn't think of that either. Perhaps it was still thought that this was the role of the woman. Women religious confessed that celibacy for them consisted principally in giving up the possibility of children. Men often didn't think about children until suddenly they discovered they were about to be fathers. Celibacy appeared to be not so much the culmination of a process we had been consciously involved in but a state we suddenly arrived at.

As students in Rome we were unusual in seeing three popes. Pius XII died at the end of our first year and Paul VI succeeded John XXIII before we began our final year. As John was the Pope of the Council, he was also the Pope of our time in Rome. He died at Pentecost 1963 and was buried in red, not black, vestments. This seemed fitting for he had lit a flame of renewal not only in the Catholic Church but throughout the Christian world. We took from him the need to open the windows of the Church and let in the Holy Spirit. His successor was neither traditionalist nor progressive. When Cardinal Montini of Milan, who had been Pius XII's Secretary of State, gave his first blessing as Paul VI with his northern accent, the man beside me in the piazza said: '*Dio mio, è francese*' (Oh my God, he's French). Unable to go forwards or backwards he became known as Hamlet.

On my ordination card I quoted the Second Letter to the Corinthians (Chapter 5) to the effect that I considered myself as an ambassador for Christ. We had a simple viewpoint of being better able as celibates to serve the community. We would discover that it would take more than diplomacy to make an impression on a rapidly changing world. A French description of a priest was '*masculin, neutre, autre*' – male, neutral, different. The public probably has some general idea about this: a priest is seen as masculine but not the usual kind because he is not married. He has to all intents and purposes been neutered. He is 'another Christ'. The Church tries to compensate for all this by making ordination to the priesthood comparable to marriage. For the priest the bride is the Church. He is the manly man of God. He is the 'Father' of the flock. Marrying would mean having to resign from the priesthood. In this way celibacy, not obedience and certainly not poverty, became the defining feature of the Catholic priest.

31

'Father'

Standing at a bus stop a clergyman of another denomination (both of us wearing Roman collars) whispered in my ear: 'Call no man Father.' He was referring to the words of Jesus as recorded in Matthew 23:9. It is interesting how many Catholics ignore this saying. I never introduced myself as 'Father'. If people gave me this title I would in return call them Mr or Mrs. They thought that was ridiculous. Yet it has to be admitted that the title does give a signal of being a member of the club. I was part of the institution. To be addressed as Mr would put one on one's guard. At the same time one had to be careful that people weren't saying 'Father' just to gain a favour. I remember bring amused by an Orangeman selling raffle tickets. When I thought to excuse myself by saying I was a Catholic priest he said, 'We're all Christians, Father!'

One of the first things I was asked to do after I became a priest was to give a talk on marriage guidance. This I declined to do, saying that I knew nothing about the subject. Marriage had been described as a 'licence to love'. Many couples decided they didn't need a licence any longer: they needed a sexual apprenticeship which was anathema to the Church. It was said men looked for sex thinking love might follow whereas women looked for love knowing sex would follow. 1967 was hyped as 'the summer of love'. The truth was that, despite (because of?) the 'bonds' of marriage many women after marrying became once more friends with their mothers while the men continued to go out with their pals as one of 'the boys'.

★★★

On study occasions provided for the clergy the main focus was the meal with preprandial drinks – although some were teetotal

members of the Pioneer Association. In my first parish the meetings were presided over by Bishop 'Jimsy' Ward, a notorious
conservative. A priest would be nominated to read a paper, briefly
it was hoped. On one occasion a junior cleric disagreed with a
comment made by the bishop. There was stunned silence. One
of the bishop's assistants intervened to diffuse the situation with a
joke. On another occasion when the younger clergy were talking
about birth control Bishop Ward asked me if I knew the difference
between burgundy and claret. He felt that would stand me in better stead. Meanwhile in parliament there were private members'
bills about abortion and homosexuality.

Bishop Ward stopped reports from the Second Vatican Council
by an American observer from being published in the local Church
paper. 'Jimsy' didn't want to know about theories of evolution or
moves towards religious freedom. The Church historian Clifford
Williamson noted that 'the more socially radical Catholics were
anxious that the liturgical innovations of the Council would lead
to reconciliation with modern social trends. The issue that provoked a breach in the Church was the heart of youth rebellion:
sex'. The Newman Association was unsuccessful in providing
reform within the Church for the growing numbers of educated
Catholics. A group opposed to clerical paternalism met in the
backroom of a Catholic bookshop. Ward remained paternalistic,
opposed to newer movements in the Church, but incredibly, on
land at Cardross near his home town of Dumbarton, was responsible for selecting the most avant-garde architectural practice in
Britain – Gillespie, Kidd and Coia– for the new seminary building
at Kilmahew, which went on to be described as Scotland's most
outstanding modernist building. Coia was an Italian Catholic who
lived next door to the diocesan offices.

In 1968, the year of protests in university campuses, Pope Paul
VI published a document called *Humanae Vitae* about marriage
and specifically birth control. He declined to follow the advice of
the commission he had set up to study the issue. It had concluded
there was no scriptural ban on artificial contraception. It was a
matter of Church tradition. Pope Paul decided the tradition had to
be maintained. Papal prohibition came as a surprise to many of us
who had begun to assume that birth control was necessary. There
was little if any warning that a prohibition was coming. Priests
were given no preparation. The following Sunday I took off my

vestment before preaching. I wanted to make the point that I was getting the information in the same way as everyone else – from the newspapers. We had been sent out from the seminary like amateur electricians who hadn't been taught to use a circuit tester; I think we did learn something on the job, as it were.

***

At the time, as part of my psychology studies, I was on a placement at Gartnavel Royal Mental Hospital. The great guru R.D. Laing was still influential there. As a psychiatrist he believed that the new consumer society created a false sense of identity because of the selective inattention it fostered. He tried to treat his patients without resorting to drugs. In the 1960s there was heavy use of drugs in mental hospitals, especially Largactil, otherwise known as 'the liquid cosh'. One day a furniture van arrived. A staff member joked it was the drug delivery.

The Gartnavel staff were bemused by the papal document on contraception. Catholics definitely were different. I took the view that it didn't make sense but it didn't impinge on my work. It was presented to us as a test of the infallibility of the Pope. But it was in fact about sex. The impression given was that, somehow or other, celibate men knew more about family life than married couples. We might not have known it at the time, but the encyclical was the end of such hubris. It proved to be the last straw for many priests, some of them recently ordained. As part of the fallout from the encyclical it is reckoned that almost 10 per cent of clergy officially applied to leave. One of those ordained with me left and was followed later by two others. However, the majority of the clergy dealt with it as a continuation of the status quo.

The clergy come in all sorts of shapes and sizes. Some are teachers, others secretaries. There are chaplains to royalty and there are hermits. There are politicians and guerrillas. Some are good at sports while others watch TV. I used to think most of the priests I lived with were quite content. But it was always possible to identify priests who were bullies, depressed, hyperactive, lazy, anti-intellectual or overly self-effacing; on reflection it is possible to see that they were dealing with celibacy in different ways. Even relatives of priests thought them immature. In turn some priests looked down on women and treated the laity as children. They may have compensated with a devotion to the Virgin Mary. Language about God was still unthinkingly masculine.

After I left Broomhill the parish priest, a keen football (i.e. Celtic) supporter, told the congregation that that was the end of what he considered to be Protestantism in the parish! One of the parishioners was the Celtic FC doctor. I went on retreat to the Benedictine abbey at Pluscarden, where the retreat master said he knew about me since one his friends in the parish (a veterinary surgeon) had complained to him about my general opinions. There was a phenomenon that some Catholics who were very active socially turned out to be religiously conservative.

While studying at Glasgow University I received the Maiden Speaker's Prize at Queen Margaret (Women's) University Union, possibly because, while wearing a clerical collar, I began my speech with: 'Unaccustomed as I am to raising my voice in a woman's chamber . . .' I was speaking on behalf of the Distributist Party. This was supposed to follow the ideals of G.K. Chesterton. The University Labour Party was thought to be too left-wing for practising Catholics. Glasgow University debating societies were run by people with political ambition and many speakers went on to distinguished careers like, in my time, John Smith and Donald Dewar. The president of the Distributist Party ended up in the House of Lords. I remember him at the end-of-year dinner telling us, to my astonishment, that the recent winning of the European Cup by Celtic FC would do more for Catholic advancement than the Second Vatican Council.

Football was an enormous business in Scotland. In Parkhead, Celtic Football Club was booming, winning everything in sight. Although I played five-a-side football with the teachers when I was in that parish, I did not go to matches. So I was deputed to take the evening services during Lent. As major matches started at the same time, a great roar erupted from the stadium while a handful greeted the priest in the church. I was only once in Celtic Park – to help with the visit of a boy who had special needs. We were well received by the staff. I knew a woman who was a secretary at Rangers. She arranged a similar welcome at Ibrox Park for the boy.

The popularity of football was not unrelated to sex. It is often said that drink sublimates. Some priests dealt with celibacy through drink but I suspect a greater number relied on Celtic for their highs. I never had much doubt that some of the Catholic clergy sublimated their sexual energy by supporting Celtic and praying that Rangers would lose. A rare example of a priest grabbing the headlines by 'running off' to get married was one who did so with the wife of a Celtic footballer.

Although celibacy is clearly a very different thing for a woman, religious Sisters dealt with it better than the clergy. My own relationships with women were with nuns. They were more involved in social ministry than priests. In my first five years, in a well-off West End parish, the most prominent person was Sister Mary Agnes, the head teacher in the private primary school beside the church. She was unusual in being an active member of the Girl Guide movement for the activities of which she had no scruples about dispensing with her veil. Although she was older than me she was the first person I fell in love with. She was a lot more sensible than me. I think the highlight of our romance was a visit to Iona. To fit in the journey within a day we had to leave the parish at 4 a.m. and didn't get back until midnight. It is impossible nowadays for people to imagine the daring that was involved in planning such an escapade.

The stiff upper lip which had prevailed in Britain had begun to loosen. *Beyond the Fringe* was an irreverent look at social habits by ex-public schoolboys. It was followed by *That Was The Week That Was*, which mocked political figures. These public attitudes had an effect on the Church. The decline in church attendance became noticeable especially, as early as 1970, among the younger. Older people remarked that youth didn't seem any worse for not going to church. The fall-off in confession was even more noticeable. My first parish priest told me that his niece in Switzerland said the priests there weren't interested in sexual peccadilloes. They wanted to know if you were uncharitable or not. Hardly anybody went to other services like Benediction. The women who had previously attended had taken up line dancing.

The practice of regular confession was one of the characteristics of pre-Vatican II Catholicism. In my first year as a priest there was not enough time to hear the confessions of all who wanted to go before Midnight Mass at Christmas. At a time when talking about sex was taboo it was a main item in confession. So it was no surprise that as the taboo lifted so did confession decline. The name was changed to the Sacrament of Reconciliation but, unlike the Mass, the format did not change. Ironically it is now confessions played out in public and usually about sex, that keep the media going.

There were several priests studying in universities at the same time as me. One of them complained that I switched to psychology to avoid being sent to the seminary to teach. It wasn't my decision that psychology was not thought to be a suitable subject for teaching in a seminary. The priest who complained about me went to the seminary to teach English but then left and got married. Previously faith and sexuality had been bound up with each other. In the 1960s these two issues began gradually to drift apart. Sex, irrespective of whether you were married or not, became a main topic of conversation. How anyone could remain celibate began to be raised as a question.

32

Second Vatican Council

It was the Swinging Sixties. The cry was 'Make love, not war!' Mods and Rockers fought over clothes styles. The prophet of the counterculture was the Lebanese-American poet Khalil Gibran, who suggested peace began in the individual. 'Amazing Grace' was top of the pops. As the poet Tom Leonard put it: God was in a tin on the shelf that could be dipped into at any time. Feminism emerged. Paternalism was out. Reform-minded Catholics discussed how the Church might be reconciled with modern trends. Inasmuch as these were about the sexual revolution they were bound to be frustrated. What the clergy hoped for from the laity was a bulwark against secular ideology.

The president of the United States could wear a 'bum freezer', the same jacket as other men. But the clergy retained the clerical collar. It was the nuns who moved into modern clothes. It was reported that one older sister, when putting aside the habit she had worn all her life, expressed for the first time regret that she had broken off an engagement before joining the convent. Among the hundred nuns resident in the Convent of Notre Dame were many experienced teachers. At the Teacher Training College they had the responsibility for teaching the teachers. Along with the Sacred Heart Convent at Craiglockhart Training College in Edinburgh, the Notre Dame Sisters in Glasgow were responsible by their preparation of teachers for making some impression in Scotland of the teaching of the Second Vatican Council. The new approach advocated by the Council was by and large resisted by the clergy. The leading Notre Dame expert, Sister Laurence, was removed by clerical manoeuvres from the Teacher Training College and exiled to Belfast because her teaching was thought to be avant-garde.

Once when, as an educational psychologist, I had to go to a school to see a client I was warned that the social worker was a nun. I wondered what they would have thought if they had known the psychologist was a priest. For myself I kept the two roles apart. I was asked if it was worse being introduced to strangers as a priest or a psychologist. The latter was probably worse because it drew the response: 'Oh, you can see inside my head.' My expertise was strictly with wayward boys. Both roles, psychologist and priest, gave exceptional access to people but it was better not to mix them up. I was never much convinced by the use of psychology in counselling. I was particularly apprehensive about being identified as a 'priest psychologist', which sounded sexy and provocative. At the same time I can't deny being a psychologist gave me some independence. One of my friends thought it enabled me to lead two lives. The parish priest amused himself by telling a visiting priest to keep his trouser flies fastened because, he said, 'Slavin always has women in his room!'

One of the assistant priests turned out to be particularly poorly suited to the role. A parishioner came to me alleging that he was having an affair with her, and once, when I thought I was taking a night call from the hospital, I overheard him on the phone talking about the IRA. I later checked his room, and sure enough there were guns under his bed. I spoke to Tom Winning, at that time the auxiliary bishop. He thought I should see the archbishop. Scanlan, a Sandhurst military graduate, was horrified. As happened in those days the priest was transferred to another parish. Nobody thought a priest could simply be dismissed. When members of an IRA group in Glasgow were arrested, someone in the police who, for political reasons, did not want to see an Irish priest in a Scottish court, tipped him off and he disappeared. We later heard he got to Ireland in a horsebox on a boat busy with Grand National traffic. After Scanlan's death I was asked if I could help rehabilitate this priest, but I didn't think that was any of my business.

The Second Vatican Council was really a preparation for putting the Catholic Church's house in order. It was based on the common priesthood of all who had been baptised. One of the main drivers of the Council was to acknowledge the debt to other Christian churches, especially with regard to the importance of sacred scripture. The fundamental role of baptism which was common to all the churches was also emphasised by the Council. It would be fair to say that up to this point the relationship among churches was that of rivalry. Once I had to explain to the archbishop why I would not, as was the custom at the time, re-baptise converts previously baptised by a Church of Scotland minister (I considered that one baptism was all that was needed). He was unconvinced but, interestingly, did not insist. There might have been at most polite acknowledgement among the different churches, but there was little contact. This was to change drastically. And for the better.

There was a very active Church of Scotland youth club in the East End which attracted both Protestant and Catholic kids. I met up with the youth ministers, Leith Fisher and David Lunan. Their families met with the families of other ministers every week in a large flat and I was invited to join them for soup and a chat. In turn I was able to invite them to come to St Mary's School. This was a complete knock-out. Even the school staff had never talked to a minister. It was a time when nominal Protestants described themselves as being of the 'opposite' religion.

One of the ministers was John Miller, who had decided to move his family into a tenement in Castlemilk where his wife Mary, daughter of a High Court judge, founded the famous Jeely Piece Club. Another, John Harvey with his wife Molly, opened a branch of the Fourth World Movement in the Gorbals. His friend Geoff Shaw, a Church of Scotland minister who married late, went on to become the first convener of Strathclyde Region. Another colleague, Richard Holloway, became Primus of the Episcopal Church in Scotland. We were all invited to join the Ecumenical Institute, an American evangelical group, but it proved to be too proselytising for our tastes.

Almost all of these dedicated ministers had families. It was not only having wives that made them different from Catholic priests. The marital relationship was not the whole of their emotional lives. Some of this was invested in their children. None of them would have seen the point of celibacy. They regarded the Catholic Church in Scotland as having to deal with the effects of mass immigration, from the Highlands and Ireland. It was not unreasonable that such ministry would require particularly dedicated staff like priests, brothers and nuns who were not married.

In general the Catholic Church was just too different for them to be able to engage with it coherently.

I developed close contact with a younger woman whose engagement had been broken off. It was probably a classic case of her going to a priest as a man who could be trusted. As it happened, both of us got the opportunity to work together in a school where the needs of the deprived were greater than our own. She went on to get married and have a family, and we remained friends. It is probably the case that not only alcohol and football can sublimate the need for sex, but also social action. My mind was focused on ministry and my energy taken up by it. That was enough to concentrate my mind. I must have had some delayed adolescence after spending so many years in the seminary, but, even though I did develop close relationships with women, I never felt the need to catch up on what I had missed.

Celibacy in religion has an ascetic aspect. To be authentic it has to be experienced as a call from God. The Christian celibate is called to imitate the unmarried Christ. He or she has the opportunity to do things the demands of family life might make more difficult. This was the model that was put before me. In practice it meant that the priest was at the beck and call of those who needed his help. Catholics in Scotland had previously been in dire straits. As their circumstances improved their need for clerical help became less. Catholic priests gradually became more like vicars, concerned mostly with church stuff. They found themselves preaching to the so-called converted. They were, as the *New Yorker* journalist Jane Kramer said of the Beats, 'rattling people who were too close to the shutdown and too new to the riches to listen to them'.

There is a contentious connection between celibacy and the sacredness of holy things as with, for example, the Vestal Virgins in ancient Roman temples. There is a natural awe of the holy. Some allege that there is a certain aptness that the celebrant of Communion should dress in ancient Roman vestments and be celibate. Some of this can be traced back to ideas of ritual purity in the Old Testament. I was part of a group of young priests giving a 'mission' in Glasgow University Chaplaincy which was caricatured with a headline in the student newspaper with a headline: 'No Sex Please – We're Catholics'.

Celibacy became the rule because of property. When the Church began to acquire land there was an intention to ensure it was kept for the family of the Church and not for the benefit of natural offspring. It was the way the Church was financed and how it was able to carry out its work. The first schools and hospitals were funded in that way. An early industry in England was the production of wool by the monasteries. One of the causes of the Reformation was the scandal that was caused by the Crown abusing ecclesiastical benefices to increase the income of their own families. The great pity was that the Reformation allowed certain families to take over Church lands for their own permanent benefit and to enable them to become the nobility. They have passed them on to their own kin even down to today. Monks may have failed, but they had the right idea of holding the land in common.

The risk in celibacy is that, ironically, it 'sexes up' the Church. The clerical collar which only came into fashion in the nineteenth century but is now worn even by women clergy makes priests too different. The Catholic Church suffered more than it cared to admit when young priests began to leave and were not replaced. There is an air of mystery about those who choose not to marry. The Catholic priesthood is seen as significantly different from the normal. How much of a challenge celibacy is to modern assumptions depends on how it is lived out in the world. It can appear simply as bachelorhood, or it can be a prophetical lifestyle enabling celibates to sacrifice themselves for the sake of others.

33

Purdah

I did not go to Bangladesh to avoid questions about celibacy. I felt I needed to see at first hand the pain of the developing world. I had felt their suffering in some abstract way. I'm not sure how common is a visceral reaction to the pain of others. It may reflect some self-centredness on my part that other relatives and friends felt my going away more than I might have myself. What I do remember was the physical demands of the first year in the tropics. It would be no exaggeration to say that sex was the least of my problems. Adjusting to the heat and particularly to a diet based on rice took up all my physical resources. It was easier not to have to shave daily so I grew a beard. Beard-growing clerics are sometimes thought to be more radical. For me it was only a matter of convenience.

Before leaving home I wrote on retreat: 'of things theological I am interested in little and sure of even less. But I do believe a religious interpretation of the world is the most adequate. I find Christianity a reasonable code of conduct. But above all I experience a gnawing of the Spirit that breaks the fetters that would hold me to the ways of this world. In all conscience I cannot accept a materialism that is beginning to appear as a required concomitant to the new social order.'

Although I was only 35 when I went to Bangladesh I found myself among the oldest in a group of more than 40 Italian priests and brothers. Even more surprisingly, I found that they were not all in favour of clerical celibacy. Especially in a Muslim culture, they saw that it could be a liability. Muslim men, who were entitled to up to four wives if they could afford it, thought celibacy was impossible. They suspected Catholic priests were married to the nuns since there was a convent in each parish!

It seems to me, however, that we could not have done the work we did had we been married. There were many advantages to the single state for missionary work. The married couples in other churches did not last long in the tropics, especially if they had children. David Livingstone left his family behind when he went on his explorations. One of the things that lost him the support of his Church sponsors was his remark to them that if they wanted to see real missionaries they should look to the Jesuits. One of the Xaverians imitated the Hindu holy men by establishing a monastery. The one I was closest to left the order and married a French volunteer worker but eventually came back to Bangladesh to do voluntary work. He kept in touch with the Xaverians and when he died was buried by them.

The original missionaries in the area had been from the great Baptist Mission to Bengal, founded by William Carey, a shoemaker from Nottingham. The British would not allow them to convert the locals in Calcutta. So Carey built a college in Serimpore, which belonged to Denmark. Gradually the Baptists ran out of missionary families. Celibate Catholic priests and nuns took over. One of the older Italian sisters told me that before she got on the boat at Naples the Mother Superior had told her: 'Don't forget, Sister – there are cemeteries in Bengal.'

The first Catholic missionaries to Bengal were English Benedictines. Six of them were drowned stepping into a small boat in the River Hooghly. At that time the French Holy Cross wanted to proceed from Canada into the United States. Propaganda Fide, in charge of missions, would only allow them to do this if they first sent missionaries to India, which they did. They then went to the United States, where they founded the University of Notre Dame. Not many know the connection of this iconic establishment with the Indian subcontinent. The Holy Cross congregation, Americans and Canadians, ministered in the areas of Dhaka and Chittagong respectively. Their highly esteemed men's college in Dhaka was called Notre Dame. The women's college was Holy Cross.

One striking feature of Bangladesh was the condition women and girls found themselves in. It was difficult to prevent even the poorer Christians from marrying off their daughters before they reached the Church rule of 16 years old. The result was that many Christian girls were sent away to train as nurses. This kind of work was not esteemed among Muslim families. Christian women, though a tiny minority of the population, became the backbone of the hospitals and clinics.

As in Scotland the nuns made an enormous difference, especially with respect to women and girls. When the Bengali Sisters changed into saris the Sister Provincial's uncle, a prominent lawyer, said it gave him bad thoughts. She told him the problem was his, not theirs. One of our part-time teachers, a French-Canadian nun, came from Chittagong on a boat across the Bay of Bengal. She slept overnight on the deck where she said male passengers tried to snuggle up to her. She said that was what happened in such patriarchal societies. But, illustrating how the patriarchal society could also be turned to useful account, she told me of a male colleague who, with the agreement of the parents, had taken a child out of the country for adoption in Canada by saying he was carrying the child for one of the women in the queue for the plane.

Once I had acclimatised I experienced falling in love for the second time. One of the Bengali Sisters who attended training courses in Jessore was unusually outgoing. We struck up a strong friendship. This was not always easy to manage in a very conservative and predominantly Muslim society. Although as a teacher she was comfortable in a Western milieu, she offered me a way into Bengali customs that would otherwise have been difficult to access. I visited not only her school but members of her family too. Among the most beautiful memories I have of Bangladesh is of sailing with her across the rivers between the villages where she worked. Later she was able to visit Scotland, where she was struck by the fact that Scots seemed to be eating all the time, even out on the street. She died prematurely, partly due to a life in Third World conditions but also because, as the other sisters told me, she did not want any special medical care for herself. Later I had the consolation of returning to Bangladesh to visit her grave.

Mother Teresa's Sisters of Charity brought the discipline of a new congregation when they started in Bangladesh. Delivering mail for them one day when I was visiting Calcutta I got the chance to meet Mother Teresa. I was impressed by the time she afforded me. It is not always appreciated that when she left the comfort of her boarding school to work on the streets a number of the boarding girls who quickly followed her over the convent wall were originally from the Christian villages south of Dacca (Dhaka) in what is now Bangladesh.

I wrote up my experience of Bangladesh in quarterly reports which were distributed by Tom and Teresa Super. These were later turned into a book called *Around Bangladesh*, published by Jim O'Donnell's Interpress. They express much unease concerning my experience. I had read Barbara Tuchman's *A Distant Mirror* about the chaos in fifteenth-century Europe. When I was in Bangladesh, the Muslims had just entered their fifteenth century. Somehow the date made sense. I quoted Brecht in *The Resistible Rise of Arturo Ui* about the difficulties of telling the truth. It takes, he said (and I paraphrase), the wit to recognise it, the courage to write it, the skill to use it and the dexterity to reach those in whose hands it will become effective.

The physicality of the experience in Bangladesh struck me as critical. It showed that food and clothing were not the most important things. One could be satisfied with much less of both. Vincent Donovan's *Christianity Rediscovered* provided a fresh analysis of 'mission'. Working with the Masai in East Africa he thought the most important thing to get over was the idea of humanity as such. Everyone has general ideas about gods and men. What he believed he was about was trying to get over the idea that the true idea of man for a Christian was the imitation of Christ. If you believed Jesus was divine then it also revealed that there was a humanity in God.

The Xaverian Missionaries had a motto of '*ad gentes, ad extra, ad vitam*'. This meant going to people who were far away and for a lifetime. They believed that in giving, they received. This was most true in that, even though they were single, they became part of a bigger family. They came to teach. They remained to learn. A member of the American missionary society (Maryknoll), Bob McCahill, committed himself to the vocation of helping poor children to attend hospital. The Muslims had the idea of the *fakir*, the holy man living on his own, so he gained great respect for this work. One Bengali, struck by my outspokenness, said to me: '*Jai bollen ta tik kintu bolla ucit na*' – What you say is correct but it ought not to be said.

When I was leaving Bangladesh the police asked if I had made any converts. I said 'one' and gave my own name. I had gone to help but ended up being helped to become more like the person I should have been. I may not have gone entirely native but I had gained a perspective. On my way back to the UK I travelled the old Raj road across the north of India. I saw Delhi and Varanasi (Benares) and, by chance, was privileged to see the Taj Mahal in moonlight. In nearby Fatehpur Sikri there is an inscription by the Emperor Akbar: 'Isa (on whom be praise) said: The world is a bridge, pass over it and build no house upon it. He who hopes for an hour may hope for eternity. The world is but an hour, spend it in devotion. The rest is worth nothing.' Being celibate allowed me personally to gain this focus.

34

Pelvic Theology

Soon after I came back to Scotland I was invited to the Confirmation of my youngest nieces (twins). The parish priest's sermon was about abortion. This was the first time I had heard the subject raised during a church service. In the UK abortion was legalised in 1967, ostensibly to deal with backstreet abortions. It was opposed by many and especially by the Catholic Church. This was not, as was claimed, about the sacredness of life. Some foetuses fail to come to full term naturally. No theological explanation was ever offered for that and little pastoral support was given by the Church to those affected by pre-term loss. The objection to abortion was that it offered opportunities for sex without the risk of pregnancy.

The sexual changes taking place were enormous. Sex-related publications became more obvious. Anything which was regarded as pornographic had previously been kept on the top shelves of shops, or out of the way. The biggest factor was the birth control pill, gradually available since the 1960s. Abortion became important as a back-up to failed contraception. This kind of freedom was a main plank in the sexual revolution which promised women control of reproduction, but it still put the onus on women as the ones responsible for the prevention of conception. Another consideration was the extension of menstruation, which was starting earlier and lasting longer. Sex for seniors became a topic of conversation. This led to the greater sexualisation of girls and older women. It extended the years of sexual activity that had the risk of pregnancy.

The Catholic Church attempted to keep a taboo on sexual matters. It became known as gynaecological or 'pelvic' theology. In the preparation for Vatican II some of the bishops wanted issues like contraception and divorce dealt with. The issues of war and peace were taken up but subjects related to sex were kept firmly off the agenda. Similarly in the 1971 Bishops' Synod in Rome on the priesthood there was no discussion about celibacy. In 1981, the Synod on the Family, there was no mention of subjects like sterilisation or artificial insemination. This blanket ban backfired. These were precisely the subjects that were beginning to dominate the public forum. It meant for many believers the opening of a gulf between their faith and their behaviour. It was often faith that was sidelined. There was a clash between liberal politics and conservative doctrine. It sometimes appeared that the only thing some of the churches were interested in was to preserve the teaching about sexual matters. 'Religionising' one part of life threatened to secularise the rest of it.

The roots of the sexual revolution lay in the scientific discourse around the beginning of the twentieth century. The better-off took advantage of the changes before they percolated down the economic scale. Scotland is more conservative socially than England, so it took a generation for the widespread changes in England in the 1960s to become popular in Scotland. In the 1980s it was clear that fewer men were embracing the celibate priesthood. It had become an issue that people were able to talk about. A poll revealed that one third of Scottish Catholics would accept married clergy. When the prominent priest Adrian Hastings married in Aberdeen, Bishop Conti removed his sacramental licence but said he would still be welcome in church houses.

Attendance at church dropped visibly. What World War One had done for the Anglican Church, World War Two did for the Church of Scotland. It was said there were no atheists in the trenches but when men came back from war many failed to see the point of going to church any more. Now the Catholic Church too was beginning to run on empty. Catholics who had acquired health and wealth found other things to do on a Sunday. There was talk of 'cafeteria Catholicism', which meant people could pick and choose the bits they wanted, like Christenings and First Communions .

It is sex that puts people off religion. It is the most personal part of life, a powerful impulse that is only managed by great effort. It is not an area where people find it easy to brook interference from others. Young people experience this first as they seek to deal with masturbation. They feel their inmost feelings are being checked by others. They suspect adults are telling them not to do as they do. This fuels accusations of hypocrisy. The situation was well summed up in the title of David Lodge's 'Catholic' novel: *How Far Can You Go?* The Catholic Church was always going to find itself in difficulties in this respect. As a fairly old-fashioned organisation it kept repeating itself as if the sexual revolution had not happened. It did have serious philosophical and theological reasons for its views but these were seldom aired. There just appeared a succession of prohibitions against any change.

Religion and sex became entangled – to the mutual loss of both. In the Justice and Peace movement there had been a group dealing with women's issues. It was difficult to persuade women that the Church would take their concerns seriously. Many women lost interest in the Church for reasons related to feminism. Many felt they were dealt unjustly by the Catholic Church. It was certainly the area where Justice and Peace initiatives made the least headway. Nobody meant to say that sex operated only on the animal level. But it seemed to be the part that the Church took the most interest in.

When there were lots of priests in Scotland it seemed natural that several of them should live together in the same house since they were single. In fact, often that didn't work too well. They were probably all too individualistic. Essentially the house belonged to the parish priest and the rest had to make do as best they could. Most could hardly wait till they became parish priests themselves. By my time this meant they would probably be living alone. Presbyteries became bachelor pads. Some parish priests, however, realised they only needed part of the house and made the rest available for parish work. The first priest I stayed with after returning from Bangladesh I thought I knew well enough to live with. I didn't know he already had a family staying with him. It became clear that keeping this family happy was his priority. Not many took a family into the presbytery with them.

The nuns I had known before going overseas were now beyond the age of reproduction. They mostly confessed that not having a child was the biggest cost to their vow of celibacy. In this they differed from male religious whose self-denial would have centred quite simply on a lack of sex. What these women missed was friendship, whether platonic or not, which might take the place of marriage. The nuns were ahead of the priests in tuning in to the temper of the times.

One, Sister Mary Ross, had, like me, been trained as an educational psychologist. We were able to pursue mutual professional interests. At a practical level she had come to help in St Mary's Secondary School. She travelled with the groups of pupils that we took on summer camps. Each year we took a small group of boys to Iona. Our visit usually happened to coincide with a group from Wimborne in Dorset so Sister had to act as the interpreter since the speech patterns were so different. On one occasion she had to dissuade our boys from taking some of the Iona doves home with them. She visited Barlinnie and was active in Justice and Peace.

Another nun, Sister Margaret Ann Minnard, had been a PE teacher in Edinburgh. She introduced me to rock climbing on the Salisbury Crags and we went on to do the Munros together. Not only did we do all the Scottish mountains over 3,000 feet but then we also did the 'further Munros' in England, Wales and Ireland. We also did the C2C (Sea to Sea) trip by bike across the north of England from Whitehaven to Newcastle. We walked from Ardnamurchan to Arbroath in the Cross-Scotland Challenge. I had played football but hadn't regarded myself as particularly fit. She showed me the importance of having a healthy body as well as a healthy mind.

The sister of a friend, Sr Marie Chambers, after becoming a nun in Scotland, trained as a medical doctor in India. While I was in Bangladesh I was able to visit her hospital in Tiruchchirappalli in South India and see the sun rising and setting over the Indian Ocean at its southernmost point. Later she was posted to Africa, where she worked with women and children. Having visited my cousin Brother Norbert in Cameroon I was able to go on to see her in Ghana, where I got an insight into the African health scene. Later she worked in rural clinics in Pakistan. After visiting some of them we were able to visit the Hindu Kush, where we saw a polo match at Gilgit. There we met a Belgian woman who was climbing the mountains alone fortified only by hot tea and digestive biscuits.

It might have been difficult to maintain such diverse friendships had I opted for marriage. The Irish writer John O'Donohue produced a book at that time called *Anam Cara* which was translated as 'soul mate'. Friendship did not necessarily involve long-term sexual commitment, he said: it could be enhanced rather than restricted by sexual restraint. Women and men could share similar pursuits which could be physical or mental or spiritual. There began talk about an 'emotional quotient'. Previously it had been thought your Intelligence Quotient (IQ) was enough to get you through life's troubles but many men found that wasn't the case. Men had to develop their emotional quotient (EQ).

★★★

In 1985 I made a midlife retreat. My hair had gone but there was no middle-age spread. The question was how to interpret 'eternal life'. My faith was no longer 'supernatural'. My daily practice of early morning yoga allowed me to start the day upside-down. How important did the Church remain? In what sense did I really remain Christian? The contrasts in my own life were considerable: I was supposed to have a promise of obedience but was no longer told what to do; I talked about poverty but, unlike most priests, had a salary; I had made a vow of celibacy but was on close terms with members of the opposite sex.

Celibacy became one possible lifestyle among others. Why did I remain committed to it? Starting up Justice and Peace and then the Scottish Drugs Forum coupled with the pressure of prison ministry didn't leave a lot of time to develop intimate relationships. There may also have been classic Catholic guilt. The choice would have been staying single or getting married. My friends were in the throes of bringing up children. Although sex might have been possible I never thought about children of my own. It was not a vocation I felt myself called to.

Jean Genet, who wrote *Our Lady of the Flowers*, thought that if you wanted to be clean you had to get down and be dirty first of all. He told the story of the prostitute who said to the priest: 'I know what I am. I hope you know what you are.' The diary of Etty Hillesum, murdered in Auschwitz, revealed a modern Dutch woman who had lived with older men yet cultivated a mystic streak within herself. Religion could not be reduced to sexual abstinence. Celibacy had to mean more than simply not getting married. It had to be a response to the call of the Gospel.

35

HIV/AIDS

In the 1980s HIV and AIDS put the details of homosexual behaviour on the front pages of the papers. It is said that up till then Lord Pakenham, the prison reformer, thought that oral sex meant aural sex over the telephone. It took until then for such activities to become news items. The HIV/AIDS scare affected mainly, though not exclusively, homosexuals. Queers, as they had previously identified themselves, had conducted their affairs discreetly. Many knew but nobody told. They feared that being discovered would lead to loss of reputation. Later the word became 'gay'. It then became possible for homosexuals to 'out' themselves. However, not all men who did not have an attraction to women engaged in sexual activity. Some remained unsure of their sexual orientation. This would be especially true if they were celibate.

The first time I met the Dominican Friar Anthony Ross was at the Edinburgh University Chaplaincy. He was in jogging gear underneath a student. They were wrestling, one of Anthony's skills. He had been a visitor to the Barlinnie Special Unit where his understanding was appreciated by the prisoners. He encouraged the Dominicans to become involved in the ministry to HIV/AIDS patients. Some of the first drug users to be infected travelled to Oxford to speak with the Dominican priests. They quickly returned, alleging the priests must be gay as well if they worked with such patients.

The change in society's sexual behaviour was obvious in Barlinnie. When I started there were a few cells for sex offenders around the officers' desk on the second floor. They were supposed to be on protection but they were routinely mistreated by those who could get near them. This did not, interestingly, include rape or domestic-abuse convictions. It meant offences against children. There might then have been half a dozen such offenders. They were the poorest of the poor, complete social misfits. The protection label, instead of helping them, singled them out for interference with their food and being harassed by self-proclaimed 'decent' prisoners. In my 10 years this situation so changed that a whole floor and indeed later a whole prison was dedicated to them. It is still not entirely clear how prisons are meant to deal with this ever-increasing population. It has become a major part of prison work. Every day the media reports cases of older men being convicted of sex offences, most of them committed in the past. Little thought has been given by the public to the care they might require in prison because of their failing health.

There is a focus on sex abuse in religious institutions and in particular on the Catholic Church, which has not only resisted the sexual revolution but publicly challenged it. When therefore sexual abuse emerged in the ranks of Catholic clergy the Church was correctly accused of hypocrisy. In my 50 years I came across one example of such sex offending by a priest. I was part of a group who occasionally gave retreats based on modern music. One day I was told a priest from the group had been arrested at a railway station having been accused of attempting to interfere with a young man on a train. My reaction was one of disbelief. My feelings of dismay were further compounded when the bishop immediately suspended the priest. I didn't think this was fair on the basis of an accusation. It is worth pointing out that the bishop involved was a convert and familiar with public schools. He recognised at once what was going on. The priest was sent to a religious establishment dealing mostly with priests who had drink problems. Regretfully it has to be added that he joined the religious order, went to its headquarters in the United States and through further offending contributed to the first bankrupting of an American diocese.

Celibacy was partly responsible for sexual abuses in the Catholic Church. Celibate sex offenders may be unusual. Researchers say that up to 75 per cent of sex offences are committed in the home. Twenty per cent are committed by children. The problem in the Church was the covering-up of the problem by men who were not married, which meant essentially there was no help available from others better qualified. Instead there was naiveté and misplaced loyalty to the institution. Hindsight is the most deceptive of visions. People are now applying the highly sexualised antennae of today to a situation where there was relatively little sexual awareness. Because priests were celibate it was difficult to know if one of them was inclined to homosexuality. It was thought that this was something that occurred in public schools. Was it not called (by the French) the English disease? Even those with a classical education probably weren't aware of the prevalence of pederasty among the Greeks. In a recent biography of the famous climber Mallory it is said that when he couldn't make up his mind about which of two young men he preferred, Lytton Strachey advised him in a letter to get on with it and rape one of them.

It is assumed that bishops moved priests from parish to parish because of sex abuse. Priests got moved around when it had nothing to do with sex. In fact, it was one of the things bishops did. It was a way of maintaining a general discipline. They regarded this as an episcopal prerogative. The bishops took advice only from senior clergy when making appointments. They were unlikely to listen when complaints came from lay people. Some parents didn't believe children who were abused by clergy. But some did complain and were ignored. Some bishops when faced with sexual misbehaviour by a priest thought that putting him elsewhere would solve the problem. They had little, if any, idea of the nature of paedophilia.

Lord Tebbit thought the cover-ups of the past were unconscious. 'It was what people did at the time,' he said. Men, when left to themselves, are inclined to mischief. They need women to temper their behaviour. The Catholic Church is particularly guilty in this respect. The 2009 film *Doubt* showed that a determined nun can prevail over the clergy when such issues arise. What has to be tackled in the Catholic Church is the difference between celibacy and bachelorhood. For too many priests celibacy has offered a comfortable bachelor lifestyle. Celibacy is reduced to being not married, a way of avoiding the liabilities of married life. There is a supposition that priests, unlike ministers of other churches, are more available to people. Anyone familiar with the heroic lifestyle of some married ministers – to say nothing of the selfless contribution of their wives – knows this to be wildly inaccurate and quite unfair. What celibacy probably does is to allow Catholics to feel more possessive about their priests than other denominations about their ministers. Catholics do feel the priest is at their beck and call. The fact that presbyteries are built next to the church so that the priest lives 'over the shop' reinforces this. This may work in a mission country. It is not so effective where the Church is established and the clergy have become part of local life.

In 1989 I found myself once more living in a presbytery. A new unit was set up for HIV/AIDS patients across the road in Ruchill, the last of the infectious diseases hospitals in the city. I took over the chaplaincy which included the geriatric wards. The archbishop, who was happy for me to serve the prison from a council flat, wanted me in a priest's house for hospital work. 'In case of emergencies,' he said. The Ruchill presbytery had separate quarters intended once for a housekeeper which were made available to me. This saved me from having to report daily to the parish. There was an excellent medical staff at the hospital, including the senior nurse, Jim Black, who became a friend. Because some of the infected patients had been drug users it was easy enough for me to visit and help them. I was also able to speak with most of the gay patients despite the Church's attitude to them. For the first time I had a call from the seminary asking if I could offer training. I asked if it was about visiting the geriatrics in the other part of the hospital. But what they had in mind was trying to get the Church's foot in the AIDS door.

Groups for sex addicts (SA) began to appear in addition to A(lcoholics) A(nonymous), N(arcotics) A(nonymous) and G(amblers) A(nonymous). SA behaviour ranged from serial dating to an obsession with pornography. Not all sexual behaviour was liberating. Abstinence, at least temporary, was recommended as part of the cure for such conditions. AA came out of the Christian background of its founders. With its emphasis on a Being greater than oneself and examination of conscience it is a model of what the Church could and should be. Many churches give hospitality to such groups. The churches could learn a lot more from such groups. It would take SA some time to build the reputation that AA had.

Celibacy should be rooted in a sense of abstinence. For some it can become a way of life which embraces not only sexual abstinence but control over eating, drinking and other behaviours that are prone to excess. When I lived with a Bengali family they were unwilling that I should share their cooking. They were Christians but the pot was strictly for family. I was expected to eat separately.

The kitchen is a place not only of nutrition but of love. Food and drink therefore have a meaning apart from nutrition. This has been explored by the Dominican theologian A.F. Méndez-Montoya as *The Theology of Food: Eating and the Eucharist*. World hunger exists in a context of comfort eating in other parts of the world and the global business of processed food. We need to connect physically to our use of food. We enjoy eating out while in much of the world mothers still cannot feed their own children. Amongst ourselves people often say that they are starving. Clearly they are not. Most of our eating and drinking is powered by habit reinforced by the artificial taste added by the food and drinks industry. When we say 'what's cooking' we mean more than we intend.

The key Christian sacrament, the Eucharist, is about food and drink. It is only the elements of bread and wine we get a taste of at Communion. But it is enough to allow us to regard all food and drink as sacred, something we should always give thanks for, say a grace over. Alcohol, though part of the Catholic sacrament, remains an enormous problem, not least in Scotland. We spend more on booze than on bombs. In Bangladesh ordinary men did not drink alcohol although the rich had access to it. Curiously, in the villages it was left to the Christians to provide it illegally. We needed some for the Eucharist but had to extract it from raisins. The Eucharist has political connotations. Some churches offer tea and coffee after Communion but the Communion itself should be enough to promote community.

Food and drink as well as nourishing people can make them sick when the taste sensation is greater than the nutritional function. Our standard of living is now based on food- and drink-related wants rather than physical need.

In 1996 I made my annual retreat at Lendrick Muir, which was a centre for holistic health. It was important to them to integrate food and exercise into the spiritual life. One of the problems in Catholic retreat houses was that they were very generous with food and allowed relatively little time for exercise. I was reminded of the inscription from Juvenal inscribed on the swimming pool in the Scots College summer villa: *mens sana in corpore sano* – a healthy mind in a healthy body. It was not a direction merely for sport. In religious life the physical and spiritual should be kept in tandem.

Once on a visit to Kathmandu from Bangladesh we were walking on one of the local trails when we saw a tea house with a white man within. We reckoned it would be a good place to stop. He turned out to be an Australian nurse who spent six months of each year working at home then the other six months doing dope in Nepal. Feeling a little sorry for him we offered him some chocolate. He looked horrified. It was the afternoon and he said he never ate anything after lunch. This made a lot of sense. 'Breakfast like a king, lunch like a prince and supper like a pauper' was an old saying. Only the need to get to work early had upset the natural rhythm of filling up before expending energy. Later on I met drug users who had perhaps a packet of crisps during the day. They looked on me as if I was nuts when I spoke of the silliness of filling one's stomach before going to bed.

The Catholic Church describes itself as the Body of Christ. It is a physical, not just spiritual, thing. Celibacy, whether temporary or permanent, is a political choice. It is comparable to the choices we make around food and drink. It is not easy to extricate oneself from the industrialised meals that come to us on an apparently never-ending conveyor belt. The connection between sex and other kinds of nourishment is intriguing. With the surfeit of sex on offer, sexual abstinence is only part of the response to the modern world. We are more than physical entities. However we define 'spiritual' there is more to human beings than what we can see. This applies to the married and unmarried alike.

HIV/AIDS brought death to the young just when we thought infection had been overcome. At this time my parents both died in advanced years. My father died suddenly at 85. We thought my mother would have enjoyed some peace and quiet but she depended on him more than we thought. She had three years as her mind gradually dissolved before dying at 88 as a result of a fall. It was difficult to accept her frailness but she enjoyed this last part of her life with the Sisters of Nazareth. Much harder to accept was the premature death of my closest friend, John, whose family had to deal with his Alzheimer's. My cycling companion Jim also died before his time. He had suffered a heart attack while cycling with me in the countryside and had survived thanks to the prompt attention of the rural GP, only to have a repeat a few years later. These deaths together with the effect on their families reinforced my belief that I was destined to remain single.

36

Psychologist

The Centenary Conference of the British Psychological Society (BPS) was held in Glasgow in the year 2000 and I was asked to say grace by my friend Tommy MacKay, president that year. Leading Justice and Peace and then the Scottish Drugs Forum, with half my time spent in prison work, I had not had the opportunity to do much professional psychology work since Bangladesh. However, I had kept up my registration and attended events sponsored by the BPS, of which I remained a member. An annual conference in Brighton stands out in my memory for the influence of alcohol upon me as I tried to win a wine-tasting competition.

Psychology offered a number of holistic possibilities for better living for everyone. I joined the newly formed Health Psychology Division of the BPS. It was my hope that it would take an interest in addiction issues. The members did not, however, see them as a health issue but rather as a social one. They were more interested in rehabilitation after hospital treatment and the like. There was a class issue. Many of the sweet young things going into health psychology had no experience of social problems. One thinks back to the original IQ tests in the USA which determined that 95 per cent of 'negroes' were morons and had found European Jews not to be as intelligent as 'white' Americans.

Like most organisations Fern Tower Adolescent Unit, part of the legendary Notre Dame Child Guidance Clinic founded in 1931 by Sister Marie Hilda, was beginning to see young people who were affected by drug problems. I was offered a part-time appointment to work with these troubled youngsters. They were already smoking and drinking and had a dreadful diet. A significant number were boys with single mothers. Several of them could have been convicted of domestic abuse for the way they treated their parent. Sexuality is not just about reproduction. It affects the person and relationships in all sorts of ways. Many of these boys lacked a father figure yet they managed to imbibe a macho culture which determined much of their behaviour.

I tested as ISTJ on the Myers-Briggs, meaning I was a sensitive, thinking but judgemental introvert. This kind of person tends to be consistent and conservative, suited best to a managerial role. This is accurate for me in that, in accordance with the typology, I compensated for my introversion by judging others and even pressing my opinions upon them. My private reactions to events were often vivid and intense although I didn't usually let that show. The career recommended for ISTJs is one where organisation is valued. I was regarded as a good organiser. My response to difficult situations was to manage the fall-out and get everyone back to 'normal'. What did celibacy add to this ability? It offered a certain detachment where one wasn't pressurised by family worries or made subject to favouring some over others.

After helping a young man from St Alphonsus parish to make a success of going to Oxford I was able to encourage several others to take up the further education opportunities that had been denied them by marriage. These were women who gave me a handle on a rapidly changing world. One of them had thought the height of volunteering was church cleaning. After studying she became a housing manager. A mother who had dabbled in drugs became a nurse. She remarried, this time successfully. Another was unable to say she was a victim of domestic abuse until she had acquired a university degree. She went on to take charge of troubled youngsters.

The Virgin Mary has an exalted place in the Roman Catholic Church. In the nineteenth century statues appeared of her without her child. But her great prayer is the Magnificat, in which she extols her motherhood with a sense of humility. Once in a quiet convent chapel I was preaching on the hope of the Magnificat to depose monarchs and raise up the poor (Luke 1:52), a woman said to me afterwards she had been governess to the King of Spain's children and he was a very fine fellow!

Diocesan priests are not monks. Monks are bound together by living out the three vows of obedience, poverty and celibacy. Local priests are closer to vicars, responsible for a congregation. Technically they are known as 'secular' priests. One of the conditions of the promise of obedience they make to their bishop is that they will not marry. They are then mostly left to get on with the job without much in the way of supervision, even from their bishop. A friend in Ireland, where priests were likely to live on their own, said about the allegations of sex abuse: 'Sure, they could have been up to anything.' The media, however, often doesn't see any difference between priests in a parish and those, like monks, in religious communities, so they are all tarred with the same brush.

A couple came to talk about their daughter. Her story had made the press because she had been seduced by her parish priest. He had already been suspended but they still needed to try and get the betrayal they felt off their chest. The Bishop of Limerick hit the headlines when he was revealed to be the father of a child. He went overseas to work as a missionary. In Scotland the Bishop of Oban too was found to have had a child. He was well regarded as a parish priest and the truth might never have been revealed if he had declined promotion. Among my own heroes the Trappist monk Thomas Merton had a midlife crisis when he fell in love with a nurse half his age. He chose to remain in the monastery. The founder of Emmaus, Abbé Pierre, had at one time to be side-lined by the organisation because of his associations with women. Celibacy clearly did not get easier with age.

The philosopher Michel Foucault attempted to write *A History of Sex* but only got as far as one volume out of an intended seven. His main point was the influence of power on sexual relations which allowed priests, for example, to use their status for wrong ends. The sociologist Erving Goffman (who did his PhD in Shetland) studied the ritual interactions of everyday life but had interesting things to say about 'total institutions' like asylums. In some respects the Church seeks to be a 'total institution' in the sense that it appears to provide an answer to all questions.

The area around St Alphonsus, since it bordered on Glasgow Green, was used in the evenings for sexual soliciting. One night a pub phoned to say a customer had collapsed on the pavement outside and needed a priest. After having given the last rites I was asked by a prostitute standing by if I required her services. On another occasion, having parked my car outside the presbytery, I was asked by one of the ladies of the night if I was there for 'business'. Another asked for a lift out of the area since she was being pursued by her pimp: we had no sooner driven off together when a police car passed and gave me a knowing look. One girl who had been sold dud drugs came in to use our phone to call the police station. She told the officer in London Road who the rogue dealer was. 'I'll get him lifted tonight,' she calmly announced to us.

I had not worn a Roman collar since I returned from Bangladesh. Now, I noticed, priests began to wear 'civvies' more often. Partly this was a response to a generally more relaxed attitude to uniforms. But it was also due to a sense that as a priest they could be *ipso facto* suspected of being an abuser. Graffiti to that effect was scrawled on church walls. I was once verbally abused in this way by some youngsters I was trying to dissuade from roller skating in the church. I told them such name-calling was a crime. 'Nae problem, big man, nae offence meant,' one of them said.

One family problem that came up at Fern Tower was the situation of grandparents who had had to take over the care of youngsters when the parents were absent due to the four Ds – drugs, death, desertion or detention. I was amazed how they managed to cope, unlike professional foster carers who could give back any difficult children. I got the chance at Strathclyde University to do postgraduate work on kinship care under Professor Hugh Foot. My model was that of Alfred Bandura, the American psychologist, on his work on self-sufficiency. His insight was that, faced with a new challenge, some people seem able to find new resources.

I knew going back to study would not be easy. Once I had 11 call-outs to Yorkhill Hospital in as many days. I had to leave Fern Tower one day to tell Transco where to lay the new gas pipe for the church so we could do away with the oil tank. I should have been more honest with myself that I liked the day-to-day busy-ness. The best part of the study was meeting the grandparents in their homes. One told me she had got an invite with her disabled grandson on to a Tall Ship. Only when she was on board did she find out she had to climb the rigging with the boy! I had the opportunity to attend a Grandparents Conference in London. This was not so helpful. These English grandparents had lost contact with grandchildren. This could have been simply through distance or because of custody disputes. Our Scottish grandparents had the opposite problem – often the grandkids had been simply dumped on them.

It proved difficult, but I succeeded in getting the 50 foster parents I needed for a convincing study sample. The questionnaire came from researchers in Berlin. Fern Tower managed the statistics. Professor Foot only commented on the methodology. Eventually I managed to hand in what I thought was a pioneering piece of research on kinship care. At the two-hour viva one of the examiners was happy enough but the other wanted a greater rewrite than I had time for. I checked with a friend in the psychology department at Glasgow University. His opinion was that it was too much for an MPhil, which was what I had submitted it for. He thought it would take a lot of work to convert it into a PhD, which I hadn't thought about. Eventually I reduced it to a paper for the BPS. It didn't take long for kinship care to become a hot political potato. Local authorities were not keen to pay grandparents for what hitherto they had taken on freely as a family responsibility.

★★★

In St Alphonsus I had worked hard. That was what people expected of me. Though when I left I said to the archbishop: 'You know I bust my butt there. If I hadn't bothered my arse that would have been all right as well.' To try and keep a sense of perspective I always had a spiritual director, first the Dominican Columba Ryan, then Gerry Hughes and other Jesuits. One year Gerry gave me a text from Isaiah 30: you 'shall hear a word behind thee, saying, This is the way, walk [. . .] in it'. It was apt advice. There is an obvious contradiction in trying to be a 'secular' priest. Is not the secular opposed to the sacred, which is what a priest is understood to be? What we should really be trying to do is to consecrate ordinary life. Celibacy lived out as a practical bachelorhood can be more of an avoidance of family responsibilities. In this way it can actually undermine spirituality. The real question for the secular or local priesthood is whether celibacy can be a virtue which influences lifestyle.

37

Men

One of the ways I dealt with celibacy was to make a deliberate effort to maintain male friends. An obvious criticism of religion is that it is old wives' tales: that the Catholic Church is used more by women than by men. But I was asked by a man if I could give him spiritual direction. I did not see myself in such a role, but I knew that there were other men in a similar situation. It might be possible to create some kind of group that could work towards mutual spiritual direction. Each of us would be supporting the others in the search for religious development.

We tried to come to terms with what it meant to be a male Christian in the middle of the current social changes. The group wasn't a church group even if the members came from a similar Catholic background. We called it 'Oneir', from the Greek word for dream. Dreaming is important in religion. The source of Jewish monotheism is the dream Jacob in the Bible had as he imagined he was wrestling with God. His son Joseph, the one with the amazing technicolor dream coat, was a dreamer. As was St Joseph, according to the account of Jesus' birth in Matthew's Gospel.

Meetings were arranged weekly during term times. As men we found it hard to focus on the proposed subject, especially if it had anything to do with feelings. Some thought we were unable to open up with each other. Two of the members were familiar with AA. There were apprehensive that we might end up with blood on the carpet. But we persevered and reached a level of sharing that many men never manage. It was clearly not easy for the male of the species to relate to each other at an emotional level. One of my contributions was learning to bake bread to share with the group.

There was an idea that other men might be interested in this so we held a public meeting. We invited Ray Simpson from

Lindisfarne to speak about the 'Green Man' tradition of rebirth in nature. There was obvious interest but we were not able to promote our ideas any further. We had days away and annual weekends to work out some kind of programme for ourselves. This was based on the standard elements of spirituality: silence, intellectual stimulation, emotional reflection and sharing food and drink. When we heard the radical American Franciscan Richard Rohr was going to visit Dublin we went over and invited him to Glasgow. He came and filled the Oran Mor theatre, which had pioneered short dramas at lunchtime with the tag 'A play, a pie and a pint'. We offered 'A prayer, a pie and a pint'.

We heard there was another men's group in one of the parishes. They were, however, more of a church group under the direction of the parish priest. I knew of another man I thought might have been a suitable member for Oneir. He had been an unruly pupil at St Mary's School when I was there. Having come back to religion he had offered himself for the permanent diaconate in the archdiocese of Glasgow. Cardinal Winning's question to him was: 'What's in it for you?' He was so put off by this that he joined another diocese and became a prison chaplain.

Even the intellectual Jesuits were now emphasising in spiritual direction the need for emotional development, emphasising EQ as distinct from IQ. More serious questions began to arise. Miguel de Unamuno has a story of a cathedral canon who didn't believe in religion any longer but still thought his priestly life had been worthwhile. I was friends with the former Episcopal Bishop Richard Holloway and Professor of Divinity George Newlands, both of whom sought to take religion beyond Church organisation. There was a sense that the old kind of spirituality was evaporating. I attended a lecture at Glasgow University by the French theologian Jean-Luc Marion, whose sign for the ultimate mystery was God with an 'x' through the 'o'.

In 1990 Ian Willock, Professor of Jurisprudence in Dundee University, founded with a few others *Open House* magazine. He was in despair about the lassitude of his local bishop. Dundee had a sizeable Catholic population and severe social problems. Willock's idea was to harness the energy of the emerging Catholic middle class for Church renewal. He was a well-established legal figure and was able to recruit writers although he was not averse to filling the pages himself when others failed to deliver. The magazine had a touch of the do-it-yourself feel of the early *Private Eye*. When he stood down through ill health it was taken over by another lawyer, James Armstrong, who brought a more businesslike approach to the magazine. The current editor, Mary Cullen, brought experience both of the popular media and Catholic institutions. She encouraged online activity with groups like *Living Faith* in England, the *Abbey of the Arts* in Ireland and *Eureka* in Australia.

It was Mary who started me doing pseudonymous film reviews for *Open House*. Each month I chose a recent film which could have some religious or spiritual interpretation. They weren't strictly speaking film reviews, more essays on a wide range of cultural and political subjects that were connected to religion. I was one of those who believed that cinemas were the new cathedrals. I had once fallen over a friend who absentmindedly genuflected before taking his seat. The very act of entering a darkened space to lose yourself in flickering images on a wall puts the audience in a middle state between dreaming and waking. Glasgow Film Theatre showed European films which were more open to thoughtful interpretation than the wham-bam of Hollywood. Although it should be said that some blockbusters also grapple with what it might mean to 'save the world'. Friends paid for a dedication in the GFT of one of the seats in my name. Films like *Priest* (1994) were beginning to appear. A gritty realism had begun to emerge which sought to get underneath the Roman collar.

Human sexuality is conscious and unconscious. Virtue doesn't mean controlling pleasure but promoting it in accordance with reason, says St Thomas Aquinas. The Church treats sex as an animal instinct yet specialises in human worries about it. In the post-digital age it has said little about internet porn. In Italy a guy whose girlfriend decided to become a nun uploaded naked images of her. She sued him. Some men have the problem not of keeping it down but of getting it up, said Peter Hebblethwaite, a priest who married late. Women's expectations are greater than that. They are looking always to be loved.

When Louise Richardson, who was the first woman to lead St Andrews University, was made the first female vice chancellor of Oxford University she said she now had her eyes on the Vatican. A feminist Anglican theologian argued for ordination to be restricted to men because it would show their role as servants. That, she thought, might resolve the problem of hierarchy. There is a certain 'uselessness' in celibacy of which more could be made. When I went on retreat to Turvey in John Bunyan country the cook was someone the monastery had accepted from prison where he had had a religious conversion. He only wanted to be a monk. He contracted cancer and was professed just before his death. Somebody said people can be divided into two kinds: mothers with children and everybody else. Not having immediate responsibility for the survival of children can make anyone feel 'extra'. Celibates have to find their place in a superfluousness beyond basic survival.

38

Pastor

As a priest I had spent only half my time living in a church presbytery. Of that most was on my own in St Simon's. Such facilities should be available also to the parishioners who pay for them. I had long been used to a single room for my own use. It was a surprise to everyone that when St Simon's was amalgamated with St Peter's I was left in the smaller St Simon's instead of having to go to the enormous St Peter's presbytery. There was a housekeeper in St Peter's who had come to me in St Simon's complaining about the pressures put on her. She indicated that she would like to move away from Glasgow. I offered to make her redundant. Her husband thought that amounted to constructive dismissal. I was only too happy to pay out of my own pocket what he claimed was her due. The days of priests being looked after by women were coming to an end.

Her place in the presbytery was taken by the recently retired James Kernaghan. He was unmarried and had been studying for the new full-time diaconate, so he welcomed the chance to practise his pastoral skills. He was an old St Simon's boy who hadn't been sure what to do in retirement. His ordination was a great occasion for us all and he proved a real asset to both parishes. His ordination was followed by that to the priesthood of Martin Kane, who had attended St Simon's while he was working at Glasgow University. He was kind enough to write that he had been partly inspired by my ministry. A priest who had been out of ministry joined as an assistant. A new Polish congregation, the Society of Christ, sent a priest to become part of the team. I was expected each week to try and get all these very different personalities to work together. It might have been like being married to several people at the same time. I had to be reminded not to try and make the parish in

my own image and likeness as some parish priests were tempted
to do.

There was a deanery structure which was meant to enable the
priests to cooperate at a local level. But they took their cue from
the bishop and were unwilling to initiate change. They wouldn't
even adjust Mass times to accommodate each other in case one
benefited financially. Most of the time was spent trying to provide
cover for the Western Infirmary and Gartnavel General Hospital.
With fewer priests, this was becoming more difficult to provide.
The most senior priests sometimes didn't bother to turn up at
deanery meetings. There were divisions among the clergy who
were all supposed to be doing the same thing. One wondered if
all that was needed was a woman to knock some sense into these
men.

One initiative I was able to promote was adult religious education. I figured that if the Church could provide bingo and dancing
it could also offer a bit of education. Gradually this built up until
we were able to fill the church hall for a year-long series of lectures
on the 50th anniversary of the Second Vatican Council. We were
lucky to have in the parish the first lay and first Catholic professor
of divinity at Glasgow University, Werner Jeanrond, who took
part. Another distinguished speaker who agreed to participate
withdrew because he thought the subject might be controversial.
Fifty years after Vatican II! Like the Council itself, we did not deal
with really controversial issues like abortion.

I was asked to visit a young gay DJ who had a terminal illness.
His parents were very anxious that he had a church funeral. He
agreed it could be in St Simon's. It was the noisiest ever funeral,
which included feet stomping to a tune from The Mamas and the
Papas. I sat discreetly in the sanctuary without saying anything. It
got a headline and I got some local criticism. The objection was
not about burying someone who was gay but about the attendant
publicity. The real question was whether the Church was willing
to offer gay people a place while alive. In the hospital some of
the most caring staff, including a male midwife, were gay. I had
a number of male friends with same-sex partners, including one
who joined the Church through the RCIA (Rite of Christian
Initiation of Adults) programme. He didn't feel the need to tell
what nobody needed to know. Eddie Linden, founding editor of

the poetry magazine *Aquarius*, wrote about the difficulties of being brought up Catholic and gay in Lanarkshire

An ancient writer described the loss of libido as akin to being unchained from a lunatic. Society however has become more sexualised. This has made celibacy all the more testing. When I started as a priest physical contact amongst people in Scotland was quite restricted. Now at football matches when a goal is scored not only the players but also the supporters jump up and kiss each other. Men and women are both more free with their embraces. Sex education appears to be based on the premise that young people will have sexual relations as soon as they are able to. Sex takes up a greater part of the media. Pornography, it is claimed, is the most popular part of the Internet. Older men are seen more frequently in the company of younger women. One would have to be a hermit not to be affected by this. Priests get kissed as well. Yet, as John Higgs said in *Stranger Than We Can Imagine*: 'For all the tits on display a culture without communion will always be more masturbatory than sexual.' The sin is not sex but sexism.

In 2013 the seven surviving members of our year who had been ordained in Rome met in the Eternal City to celebrate our Golden Jubilees. Three were grandparents. I also celebrated my own 50th anniversary of ordination with family and friends in the parish of St George, where I had been brought up. Dom Gregory of the Turvey Benedictines was fond of saying that losing faith is part of old age and a call to a different kind of faith. The Welsh-speaking Anglican priest R.S. Thomas was considered to have an outlook that was bleak. Yet in the most ordinary things of village life he found intimations of faith, hope and love. I too found in the most ordinary things of life meaningfulness which took me through them and beyond them.

I had set my 70th birthday in 2010 for my retirement. I had reached my allotted span in good health. Now I wanted to give time to reflect on what it had all been about. Yorkhill Hospital was due to transfer to the south of the city. The only awkwardness was that Archbishop Conti had resigned but had not been replaced. I thought this would have been done quickly and I could get away. In fact it took three years. During that time there were difficulties with one of the staff of the Emmaus Community who threatened to go to an industrial tribunal. Since I regarded her as a colleague

I thought I could use our friendship to persuade her to accept an agreement. She accused me of behaving inappropriately. I resigned from Emmaus. When eventually a new archbishop was appointed he invited priests to say whether they wanted to retire or not. I was in my fiftieth year of ministry. It was time to go.

The twelve years I spent in St Simon's were the longest I had ever lived in one house. It was probably expected that I would retire there. Priests were becoming much fewer than people had been used to. It would have been a comfortable billet. Some years before, when I had finished climbing the Munros, I had decided I had had enough of using a tent. My work pension was small enough to be cashed in. It gave me the means to get a campervan. The inspiration partly came from the Russian idea of '*poustinia*', a place where one could spend time alone without being entirely cut off from others. My plan was to reduce my worldly goods to fit into that campervan. When I retired I drove off into the sunset alone.

39

Love

What if I had not gone to Bangladesh but had remained in Scotland? I had the chance before leaving to become a university chaplain. The priest who was appointed in my stead went on to become a bishop. How would I have coped with that? I enjoyed 50 years of priesthood. I am certain I would not have enjoyed being a bishop. Going to Bangladesh was a liberation. It also allowed me to have a wider-ranging group of companions and friends.

Justin Martyr made clear to his inquisitors that reading the Book or giving to the poor was not enough. The first Christians had something to celebrate on Sunday, the first day of the week, when they remembered the Resurrection of Jesus. He had commanded at the Last Supper that they took the elements of food and drink and shared them with each other. This very physical act confirmed them in love for each other. It brought about a real sense of companionship.

The stories of the resurrection of Jesus came from women, first of all from Mary Magdalene. One of the great stories of Jesus' ministry is his dismissal of those who accused a woman of having committed adultery. St Peter had a mother-in-law, so he was married. Women (and children) have a surprisingly high profile in the Gospel stories. Chastity as faithfulness to one's partner is enjoined by most religions. Celibacy came later to the Catholic Church.

When people speak of spirituality and meditation they imagine this to be Eastern in origin. The Christian faith, like other religions, has its sources in the Middle East. Pius XII, commenting on the importance of the Bible, said we are all Semites. The founders of Western monasticism like Hilary of Poitiers came from Egypt. They then built up a tradition that has had a powerful effect in the West. It was formulated as a rule of life by St Benedict, who in the sixth century built a cell for himself in Subiaco, south of Rome. Benedictine ideals since then have influenced not only learning but also the agricultural economy. Whether people interested in spirituality are ready for the challenge of monasticism is another question. We don't have to go to the East. There are monasteries in our midst offering retreats and other guidance.

Although society is full of people practising celibacy for much of the time it is a fact that one of the few people they will recognise as accepting it permanently is the local priest. This model came into its own with the powerful missionary thrust from countries that remained Catholic after the Reformation. The Spanish and Portuguese took this kind of Catholicism to the ends of the Earth. Some of them thought that with new converts they made up for what had been lost at the Reformation. Those who ran the British Empire were less keen on proselytism. Only latterly were Protestant missionaries able to enter the scene. They were followed by the Catholic missionary orders. Many came from Ireland. One of the ironic legacies of the British Empire is the establishment of the Catholic Church in its domains by unreformed Irish celibates. The role of celibacy outside the mission field is more problematical – unless one is convinced that all pastoral work is missionary.

There are two quite different reasons for celibacy. One is practical and not uncommon. Sexual partners may have to be celibate when one is absent or incapable of sex for whatever reason. Death or an accident may make people celibate permanently. Regret over the loss is personally so intense for some that no substitute is possible. For others the search for a new partner is too much hassle. The media exaggerates the importance of sex. Celibacy, temporary or otherwise, is more common than is generally admitted. When sex is not in the equation friendship is easier.

The second is idealistic and quite rare. In most religious traditions there is a different idea where sex is given up voluntarily. In Hinduism a vow of chastity releases the person from social obligations so that they are free to pursue the search of eternal truths. It is often taken later in life after one has made a contribution to society. Mahatma Gandhi was eventually able to sleep with young women without sex. In Christianity celibacy has been the role, first of all, of monks who lived in monasteries beyond the usual inhabited places. Later there were friars who went among the people with the mission of calling them back to God. In this tradition a place was found also for women. Previously they would have been married off or left in the unmarried state. The state of never having had sexual relations became the norm in female religious communities.

Women can (or, now, more accurately, used to) see priests as a safe male. However, it is disconcerting always to see a priest surrounded by women who appear in a subservient role. E.I. Watkin said mysticism is not disguised sex; sex is disguised mysticism. In the face of this the Church tries to preserve a 'monosexuality', as if we were all the same. At the same time it takes for granted male privilege. It is an environment which allows bishops to set themselves up as the hierarchy with priests as courtiers or eunuchs.

Until recently, prolonged bachelorhood and late marriage remained common among the Celts. This made it easier to recruit celibates among them into the ranks of the priesthood. It also allowed them to retain the friendship of unmarried peers. A recent American report claims that only a small percentage of Catholic priests have attained the ideal of ascetic celibacy. The secular priest mostly has a practical celibacy. The Church's need for a 'holy janitor' who will make sure the building is in working order keeps the clergy busy. The high profile of priests comes from their role as missionaries to immigrant groups, often in the midst of hostile hosts. When it becomes primarily a caretaker task it is hardly appealing to those who do not see themselves as church mice.

Today the Catholic Church requires the presider at the Eucharist to be a celibate priest. These are getting harder to find. Is it time again, as it was in the beginning, for the clergy to be married? There is now more interest and support for married clergy in the Catholic Church. In the Eastern Church men who are married can become deacons and priests. Men cannot marry after ordination. Bishops are chosen only from the celibate. In the Western Church the imposition of celibacy coincided with the expansion of monasticism in the eleventh century. It remains to be seen whether married clergy could be afforded financially. Catholics in this country are used to a Church that exists on a wing and a prayer. The current hope appears to be that enough young African priests can be persuaded to return the favour of the money that used to be sent to help 'black babies', and come to Europe. However, the modern African accent can make it difficult for them to be understood. They are also used to palaver and therefore long sermons. This is not what the average Catholic expects on a Sunday.

A significant event in Scotland was the visit of Pope Benedict XVI in 2010. There were prophets of doom but as with John Paul II the sun came out on the day. The crowd was significantly smaller this time, partly due to the new business of health and safety. But it was also a less populist event and much more carefully managed than the one in 1982. Every flag was there except the Union Jack. At the election of Pope Francis we learned both of them had been neck and neck during the 2005 election. Cardinal Bergoglio had said he didn't want it and Cardinal Ratzinger had said he would take it. One is left to wonder what Jorge Bergoglio/Pope Francis might have done had he arrived eight years earlier.

Three years later Benedict resigned and Bergoglio became Pope Francis. Scotland's Cardinal O'Brien did not attend the conclave. There was a very slight chance he could be elected. Some former students went to the press with stories of sexual behaviour with him while he was their rector. Catholics were truly shocked that as a cardinal he had spoken out against gay activities while concealing his own history. He had immediately to step down and go into exile in England.

Father Dan Berrigan SJ, the American anti-Vietnam War protester, said celibacy made it easier to go to prison. Not many of us go to prison. Celibacy should allow compassion to be unlimited. If it is not about the love of others it is nothing. It has been reduced in the eyes of some, including the celibate, to a bachelor lifestyle. Now that bachelors can have sex without getting married its value as a sign of solitary commitment is diminished. Some priests have dealt with erotic desire by physical comforts in their living conditions, or by money and drink. Sexual abuse occurred in a minority. Much more common is small-time bullying, especially of women and children. Many priests find it difficult to deal now with their lessening public status. But it is a change for the better.

Dedicated women can achieve more than male strength can. Sister Rachele Fassera rescued 110 girls who were kidnapped by the Lord's Resistance Army in Uganda. She refused to change out of her religious habit. Sister Mary McLeish SND from Scotland would not obey government instructions in Southern Rhodesia to segregate her pupils. Sister Helen Prejean, the American anti-death penalty campaigner was admired for faith in her cause. In the film about her life, *Dead Man Walking* (1996), she said faith is hard work. Sister Ilia Delio says: 'Celibacy means putting another family in front of your own.' Celibates do not know whether they would have been able to have children of their own or not.

Talk about sex has now become explicit. It is reckoned the majority of children access adult material on their digital gadgets. Sexting is a problem. What was looked down on as swearing is promoted as Anglo-Saxon language. Not the least of the difficulties of writing about life as a celibate is the detail one would be expected to go into about intimacy in order to defend one's way of life. Celibacy is meant to have an apocalyptic aspect. In a sense it is an early death sentence. But love is as strong as death – as we read in that great piece of biblical eroticism The Song of Songs. The best exemplar of celibacy today wasn't a priest or even a Catholic. Dietrich Bonhoeffer was martyred by the Nazis in the last days of the Second World War for his witness to religionless Christianity. He left behind a distraught fiancée.

Celibacy may not always be a choice. It may be the recognition of the facts of our existence. And that is whether it is a temporary situation or a lifelong choice. Rilke said: 'Staying is nowhere.' We are all always on the move. It is in the moments of transition that we get a glimpse of the divine. In a certain sense all our energy is sexual but it doesn't always need sexual satisfaction. Sometimes the acceptance of what we cannot do is a liberation. It allows our love to be passionate, even for the stranger. Our meaner needs may get in the way of our better thoughts. The media makes evident that, whether we have religious beliefs or not, sexuality is a privileged theatre of guilt. The source of that lies in the human condition. Changes in our attitude to sex require a change in our attitude to God. Otherwise our faith will get spoiled. Growing into celibacy offers a new view of unconditional love.

Carl Jung spoke of an 'infantile dependence' on externals which prevents us from developing our full potential. Aldous Huxley described the 'incessant appeals to greed, competitiveness and aimless distraction' as 'the original sin of the mind'. There is a constant battle between natural curiosity and the constant barrage of stimulation from the screens of virtual reality which surround us. Monasticism has been described as the ultimate reset button. We may well end up not only beyond our own kith and kin but with people of a different culture. In American retirement homes older women who have remained all their lives within their own societies find themselves being cared for by immigrant men.

When I started as a priest it was assumed that couples asking to be married were living apart. Now it is presumed they both have the same address. Of course there has been a big move away from asking a celibate cleric to celebrate marriage. People expect more compassion than can usually be delivered by a cleric. There is something to be said for the Napoleonic Code which even in the Catholic countries of Europe requires a couple to go to the mayor's office before they go to the church. The Church also needs to support more those who are single whether that is a life choice or a situation that they find themselves in.

One of the great insights of my life was being told that whereas women had 24 X chromosomes, men had 23 and a half plus a Y. The truth is, looking closely at it, that the last one in men is not a Y but a broken X. Men have a bit missing. Women have the full set. No wonder men are somewhere on the autistic spectrum, some further along it than others. There is also, I believe, an autistic morality among men. Sexual activity is substantially ego-based. Sexual desire is often oblivious to the rights of others. Chastity is a real virtue intrinsic to a wholesome life. It is not a thing that comes easily to men. The nature of the chromosomal make-up should make us more sympathetic to those who find it difficult to define their own gendered mood.

During the week of Christian Unity we had in Partick instituted a lunch which brought together a range of clergy from the more musical amongst us like St Bride's Episcopal to Dowanvale Free where the minister had left over the introduction of organ accompaniment. Together on Good Fridays we put up a cross in a nearby park and prayed together. It was good for the different congregations to see married and unmarried clergy working together.

The cinema may be imagined as a cathedral of the modern world where people sit in silence in the dark. No two people see exactly the same film. They come out arguing about what they have just watched. It is worth reflecting that we don't know exactly what is in people's heads when they are in church. Which might be just as well since they are not all in church for the same reason. Film today faces religious questions without God. Many modern movies seek to provide answers as to how the world is to be saved. The older films may have had low-life characters but they were full of faith, hope and charity. Audrey Hepburn said the beauty of a woman is not in her face but in her soul, in 'the caring she lovingly gives, the passion that she shows'. Antoine Saint-Éxupery wrote: 'Eyes are blind. One must look with the heart.' In his book *Solitude*, Anthony Storr quotes Kafka: 'One can never be alone enough when one writes, there can never be enough silence around one, even night is not night enough.'

In the film *Babette's Feast* (2012), reported to be a favourite of Pope Francis, two spinster sisters, after the death of their minister father, try to maintain the strictness of his Danish congregation by reading from Scripture. Gradually they all descend into backbiting. They are only saved by a French refugee who cooks them a magnificent meal from a win in the lottery. This is the importance of Communion. It is not enough to listen to words. We have to love in deed. Men and women, single and celibate, are all called to the same spirit of compassion. We have to share our bread with each other.

Having buried my parents, both having achieved the fullness of life, and beginning to see contemporaries slip away, some of them before their time, it is possible to see only the embers of faith. That is when it becomes possible to believe that from the ashes a new fire may arise. Celibacy, temporary or permanent, as a witness to Jesus has its ultimate meaning when it allows the Spirit to show clearly in the life of the celibate. The old religious mantra of prayer, penance and almsgiving should be translated today as meditation, discipline and fundraising, all of which have a modern appeal.

Afterword

Stephen Hawking asked why is there anything – rather than nothing? Religion is a response to the sense of wonder at creation. Some of the answers that have been offered for our origin and destination provoke a necessary dissatisfaction. As Hamlet said, 'there are more things in heaven and earth, Horatio, than are dreamt of in your philosophy.' Radical religion is about a sense of transcendence, of reaching beyond ourselves. In our digital world we need to keep a dimension of resurrection.

Adolescent Units exist in the psychological services to give those young people who are abusing power, money and/or sex an opportunity to stop for a moment. They are given the chance to think about what they are doing – to ask themselves if that is the way they want to continue, considering the cost not only to themselves but to their carers and others. Often with the help of staff they get a better grip on their lives and are able eventually to grow up.

There should be Senescent Units to serve a comparable purpose for older people. Some deny they are growing old. Others are tempted to live out the adolescence they feel they were denied. Pensions make this financially possible. And, if things go wrong, there is the National Health Service. Such views obscure the issue. Our lives are finite. Ageing cannot be prevented. It is a natural process. Just as young people need help with the turmoil of growing up, so older people need help to face the ultimate disturbance of growing *down*.

St Peter, that boisterous leader of the first Christians, made extravagant promises to the Risen Christ about what he was going to do to organise a Church. Jesus said to him, 'When you were younger, you girded yourself and walked where you wished; but when you are old, you will stretch out your hands, and another will gird you and carry you where you do not wish' (John 21:18). In care homes older people are mostly disempowered. Obedience, poverty and celibacy are thrust upon them. They are expected to obey the rules of the establishment. Their money is taken from them. It is presumed they have become asexual. Dylan Thomas, dying before his time from the effects of alcohol, raged against 'the dying of the light'. It should not be so with those who have enjoyed the fullness of life. The powers we have acquired, the achievements we have made, the partners and children we have cherished become – naturally – more distant to us.

We have spent our lives in an in-between state. We got a job, we made money, we had a family. It was a struggle to make a success of it. We controlled our diet, took exercise, maintained relationships. But in a certain sense we always knew that we are on our own. We are alone in the crowd. Sooner or later we wonder why we were born. Then we worry about how we are going to die. De Unamuno tells the story of an old priest in Spain who confessed to his nephew that he had no belief left – but that if he had his life to lead again he would live it in exactly the same way. 'The late period', writes Anthony Storr in *Solitude: A Return to the Self*, 'is a time when communication with others tends to be replaced by works depending on solitary meditation.'

The Book of Job tells us that when it is easy to believe, belief doesn't mean very much. It's only when it is hard that there is a point to it. The philosopher John Caputo says: 'In the head it is easy to know God as Other, in the heart it is hard to know the Other as God. God is an icon, not an idol.' It is difficult to find the appropriate language for such feelings. Jesus and/or Christ has become an epithet uttered when people get a fright or want to express strong feelings. Real prayer is like learning to talk again. Or, more accurately, it is a form of speech more basic than any other.

The main fruit of the Enlightenment was not science, which had been around for a long time. It was an understanding that the greatest thing we can do is exercise compassion. Robert McCrum, author of *Every Third Thought: On Life, Death and the Endgame* (2017), arrived at the conviction that 'the internal dialogue provoked by "every third thought" (about death) can only be resolved by narrative. Once upon a time that was the role of religion. But what kind of self-justifying stories can [people] tell themselves to sustain their resilience in an age without faith? The short answer [. . .] has been the assertion of self, in that cocktail of optimism and defiance we call willpower'.

Dylan sang, 'I was so much older then, I'm younger than that now.' We should relax and relate to whoever is around us – irrespective of race, class, colour or creed. Other people – those less well off than us throughout the world – need food and drink as much as we do. There is a monastic archetype within each and every one of us – a desire for an interior, more contemplative life. The values of the mind are patience, courage, perseverance. They are opposed to an external self based on power, money and possessions. We are invited to an asceticism of loving which means giving time, talent and treasure to others.

That great film *The Shawshank Redemption* (1994) ends with a scene reminiscent of the final chapter of the Last Gospel where Jesus meets again his dejected followers and gives them new hope. Andy, having escaped from the living death of prison by the water outflow pipe (baptism?), is mending a boat by the seashore when Red, having served his time, comes to look for his former friend. A new life is about to begin. The Spirit that seemed hardly to survive in the harsh environment of incarceration has been set free. As the Marriage Rite reminds us: divine love is explained by human love, not the other way around.

The theologian Kenneth Leech, whom I went to London to meet, described the Anglican social reformer, Canon Evans, in terms that made me think of my own strengths and weaknesses. He said Evans 'was extremely shy and covered this up with an aggressive manner which often bordered on the insensitive and cruel. In his personal ministry he was one of the gentlest men I knew. In public he was a ruthless debater and a fierce controversialist.' Evans insisted on the holiness of the common life: he totally opposed the 'Church condescending'. Evans was a living example of Gramsci's organic intellectual, a resource given for and learning from popular struggles. He had a strong commitment to the pub as a place of comradeship and pleasure.

Friends used to ask when the real Willy Slavin would stand up. They described me as an angry young man. The truth is that my various ministries took me into sensitive areas where compassion was needed. The issues being debated did not seem to me to be at all controversial. Those who looked down on the excluded – the poor, prisoners, drug users, homeless, the destitute overseas – were, in my opinion, simply wrong. I wanted to use what talent I had on behalf of those who were discriminated against. I want to say that I was helped by obedience, poverty and celibacy.

In the final decade of our existence a simpler form of life may appeal to us. We used to wonder why we were born. We begin to worry about how we are going to die. These are not questions we can answer. What we do know is that faith, hope and love can be our guide. The greatest of these is love and the bond of friendships for all, irrespective of race, class, colour or creed. Naked we came into the world – but we were believed in, we were hoped for, we were cared for. We pray to leave it in the same way.

In 'The Old Man's Comforts' Robert Southey wrote:

You are old, Father William, the young man cried

The few locks which are left you are grey;

You are hale, Father William, a hearty old man

Now tell me the reason, I pray.

At the end of the day it all has to be how we were loved and how we loved others. This must include a particular concern for others, especially the stranger. In other words, a sense of charity that amounts to real compassion, a willingness to suffer alongside others. It is a special kind of life of its own, uniting the person tangibly to a higher plane of contemplation. We are not waiting on Christ to come. He is waiting for us. Thomas Merton puts it as well as anybody: 'What I do is live. How I pray is breathe.' Religious choices can come late in life.

Envoi

After completing this book and about to enter my 80th year I was diagnosed with a tumour in the bladder, the consequences of which were treated at the Beatson West of Scotland Cancer Centre. So, as predicted, a bit has fallen off. Cancer, we are told, will affect half the population as it grows older. One of the nurses said: 'If you don't die of it you will die with it.' So I am not ill. I am a person living with cancer.